THE   BEST

CATHOLIC
2004
WRITING

THE BEST

CATHOLIC

2004

WRITING

EDITED BY

BRIAN DOYLE

LOYOLAPRESS.
CHICAGO

LOYOLAPRESS.

3441 N. ASHLAND AVENUE
CHICAGO, ILLINOIS 60657
(800) 621-1008
WWW.LOYOLABOOKS.ORG

The Bible excerpts in "The Lunatic in the Pew," "God in the Tangled Sheets," "In the Dark," and "Deliver Us from Evil" are taken from the *New American Bible* with Revised New Testament and Psalms. Copyright © 1991, 1986, 1970 by the Confraternity of Christian Doctrine, Inc., Washington, DC. Used with permission. All rights reserved. No portion of the *New American Bible* may be reprinted without permission in writing from the copyright holder.

The Bible excerpts in "The Leper: Robert's Story" are taken from the Jerusalem Bible, © by Darton, Longman & Todd, Ltd., and Doubleday & Company, Inc., 1966, 1967, and 1968. Reprinted by permission.

The quotations from Henri de Lubac in "The Present Crisis through the Lens of the Laity" are taken from *The Splendor of the Church* (New York: Sheed and Ward, 1956).

Cover and interior design by Think Design Group

Library of Congress Cataloging-in-Publication Data
The best Catholic writing 2004 / edited by Brian Doyle.
    p. cm.
 ISBN 0-8294-1729-X
 1. Spiritual life—Catholic Church. 2. Best books. I. Doyle, Brian, 1956-
BX2350.3.B48 2004
282—dc22

2004006499

Printed in the United States of America
04 05 06 07 08 09 10 11 Bang 10 9 8 7 6 5 4 3 2

In memory of Andre Dubus

Contents

Introduction

The first Catholic writing I ever committed, I now confess publicly, was a complete and utter theft from C. S. Lewis. I was maybe twelve years old and I had just read *The Screwtape Letters* and I thought old C. S. had a pretty good thing going there and I ripped him off with the blithe cheerful sinfulness of the professional editor I would someday become.

Not only did I steal from the poor man, but I stole for maternal credit—I wrote a Letter from Hell, refusing my mother admission to the Dark Gates, and slipped it under her breakfast plate on Mother's Day. My dad, who was and is pretty sharp about good writing, being a good writer and all, thought it was entertaining and creative and sent it to his friend Fr. Louis Miller, who ran a magazine in Missouri called, then and now, *Liguorian,* and Louis published it, not knowing he was a party to blithe theft, and he sent me a check for ten dollars, which I would like to say I still have, because that would be a cool writerly thing to say, but I spent it as fast as I could get it out of my hand, I think on Butterfinger bars. I had a ferocious jones for Butterfinger bars when I was a kid.

So there you have it—unadorned theft, unearned credit from my mama, a deluded dad, and way too much sugar. My professional career was launched.

That might have been the end of the whole Catholic writing thing for me, for I took the faith of my family and forebears seriously enough to soon feel like a dolt about stealing, even though I'd stolen from a Britisher, which isn't so bad, considering the slave masters they had been to my Irish forebears, but right about then I found the stories of J. F. Powers on my parents' vast bookshelves, and then I found Flannery O'Connor, and then Walker Percy, and then I wandered headlong into Thomas Merton (who never had an unpublished thought, the poor mule) and Dorothy Day (whose face looked like a mountain in Vermont) and Peter Maurin (who reminded me unaccountably of Charlie Chaplin), and then, delightfully, into Xavier Rynne's masterful *Letters from Vatican City,* and I was hooked, apparently for life.

There was really and truly something different about writing of and by Catholics and about Catholic matters, I realized, and while it was (and is) pleasantly difficult to articulate what exactly that something different was, and what exactly "Catholic writing" might be, there *was* some swirling deeper substance to it, something you could sense—the substance of things hoped for, perhaps.

I stayed attuned as the years sprinted by, and I got regular jolts of espresso writing about Catholic matters from such luminaries as Barry Lopez, Annie Dillard, Mary Gordon, Paul Wilkes, Ron Hansen, Alice McDermott, Gilbert Keith Chesterton, Andrew Greeley, Joseph Bernardin, Bob Burns, Bruce Springsteen, and even such unexpected talents as the novelist Tony Hillerman, who grew up Catholic in Oklahoma, and the extraordinary naturalist Terry Tempest Williams, whose heroine is Teresa of Avila. Most of all, for me, the late Andre Dubus, whose fame as a writer had come from his haunted and piercing short stories but whose greatness as a writer of love and grace and duress and miracle and sadness and salvation flowered late in two collections of extraordinary essays about sacrament immanent in every moment; and for your homework today I assign you Andre's *Meditations from a*

Movable Chair, which I say is the greatest collection of Catholic essays since Flannery O'Connor stopped writing letters to her friends. I believe that one of the great voices in Catholic history was stilled when Andre died in 1999, and it says everything about the wild sweet confusing depth of American Catholicism that its finest essayist was sweet, rude, devout, grouchy, a former Marine captain, a pacifist, and the father of six children. Such conundrums are we all.

But we cannot here, of all places, dodge the ancient question What *is* Catholic writing? Writing by Catholics, for Catholics, of Catholics?

Welllll: yes, yes, yes, no.

Yes: there is a startling amount of really fine writing done every year by Catholic men and women and youth. There's a kid named Anna Nussbaum, for example, who must be all of twenty years old now, a student at the University of Notre Dame, who has written two or three of the best things I have ever read from a young Catholic.

Yes: there is a remarkable amount of fine writing published every year in Catholic magazines and newspapers and journals and reviews and Web sites and books. I mean, really, it's stunning. The next time somebody tells you there is a dearth of fine writing in the Catholic press, I suggest you snort so hard your spectacles fly into the next room.

And yes: there is a surprising amount of writing done on "Catholic matters" by writers who are not Catholic, published in venues that are not Catholic. This has been especially so over the last two years, as the church has roiled and wept and raged over news of horrific rape and abuse and cowardice and sin in its midst for decades.

But no: Catholic writing is also, delightfully, miraculously, catholic. To limit a collection such as this to only material that specifically concerns churchiana would be a mule-headed mistake, for the essence and joy and struggle of Catholicism is to grapple with the largest questions of human existence: How can love defeat murder? How are we to be moral citizens of the nations in which we live? How *are* we to live? How are we to pray ceaselessly, to attend constantly to miracle, to bring our wild love to bear on the bruised and broken world?

So the purview of this volume, and, I hope, of its successors from Loyola Press, is love and death, war and peace, sin and grace, courage and cowardice, all seen through a Catholic prism. Everything, seen with a clear enough eye, is meat for the Catholic mind—so in these pages you will find scholar Scott Appleby's astringent and pained talk to America's Catholic bishops, and Chris de Vinck's gentle elegy to his late friend Fred Rogers, and Ben Birnbaum's terse account of praying while walking, and Alice McDermott's lucidly honest account of making Catholic art, and . . . well, you'll see.

All Catholic, I say.

And I am an editor and so never wrong yet.

This first volume in the Best Catholic Writing series was prepared as American Catholicism struggled through a dark sea of sex-abuse scandals, and it would be wrong to account this horrendous time shallowly, especially since there are very many of us American Catholics who pray that this acid bath will heal and restore and renew and reshape the church we love, the church we trust to help us live as if love was the nutritious and necessary bread Jesus said it was. Thus not one but three of the pieces that follow deal with this dark chapter in the ancient and eternal life of this most interesting and most remarkable faith. Sorry if that seems top-heavy, but trust me when I say the pieces are riveting, eloquent, substantive, and real. It is my fervent hope and prayer, as I am sure it is yours, that we will be a church people who never have to read this sort of piece again.

Speaking of prayers . . . it is a capital mistake to include work by the editor of an anthology in an anthology, such overweening arrogance being a venial sin and a misdemeanor in several states, but included here is a piece by the editor, for two reasons: one, it is a haunting prayer and remembrance and chant and litany and poem for the men and women and children murdered in New York City on September 11, 2001; and two, I didn't really write it. I just wrote down the line or two from the extraordinary "Portraits of Grief" in the *New York Times* that broke my heart every day, and after a while there came to be a kaddish.

I have learned, over the years, when I read or speak in public, to thank the people in attendance before we begin the unpredictable event to come, for it seems like a great gift when people pay attention to something before they even know what it is. That's true here—you have procured, through fair means or foul, this volume, and you are about to read it, and you don't know whether it will sing or be a stick in the eye. So thank you, most sincerely, for your faith in what is to come—the substance of things hoped for, as our friend the Bible says.

—Brian Doyle

The Lunatic in the Pew

Alice McDermott

from *Boston College Magazine*

I'm not a very good Catholic. I started skipping Mass as a teenager, as soon as my older brother got his driver's license and my other brother and I could pile into his car for what we would tell our just-returning-from-the-ten-o'clock parents was noon Mass, and then make a quick, hour-long detour to Dunkin' Donuts. What we complained about in those days was the church's hypocrisy, its trivial rituals and petty obsessions, stuff we thought no one else had ever noticed.

Through college, I went to Mass only on occasion and even then simply because the Newman Center at my state college had a funny priest whose sermons were pre-*Seinfeld* stand-up routines about the foibles and the excesses of campus life. I became in my twenties what my father used to refer to as an A&P Catholic—one of those Catholics who only stop into church when they need something or run out of something. I got regular and somewhat steady about churchgoing when my children were born, telling my skeptical and permanently apostate friends and family (my brothers among them) that I was giving my kids Catholicism in order to inoculate them against the Moonies and the Hare Krishnas, the occasional pair

1

of Mormons at the front door; that I was giving myself the advantage of knowing something about the religion against which, I was certain, my children would eventually rebel.

When it came time for our first child to begin school, we dutifully bought a house in a neighborhood with an excellent public school system, and it was only after we learned that our son would have a lengthy kindergarten commute because the local school was being renovated that my husband, a Methodist, suggested we look at the nearby Catholic school. On the day we were to meet with the principal, I arrived a few minutes early and took my own private tour. It was all too familiar: the uniforms, the orderly rows of desks, the crucifixes and holy-water fonts and carefully colored cutouts of little lambs and big-eyed shepherd children. The Catholic school smell, which most especially brought back the terror and the tyranny of my own Catholic grammar school, where we were fifty or sixty to a classroom and Sr. Edwina stalked the place like a long-robed Captain Bligh. I was nearly hyperventilating as I met my husband at the principal's door, prepared to say, "Let's run, let's get out of here. We can't perpetuate the madness," when he, grinning, informed me that he had also arrived a little early and had made his own tour, counterclockwise to my own. "I love this place," he said, before I had a chance to object. "The uniforms, the order, the religious symbols. We can't send him anywhere else."

Even now, I confess, my involvement in the daily life of the church is minimal: school-related activities, check writing, a meal or two for the homeless. I'll occasionally miss Sunday Mass out of laziness, or busyness, or be deterred by the prospect of sitting through yet another sermon full of half-hearted platitudes.

Even now, as I find myself expounding on a topic such as this—being Catholic—I imagine the Dominicans who taught me in grammar school or the Josephites who taught me in high school rolling their eyes or, as the case may be, rolling in their graves. I hear my no-longer-practicing Catholic friends and family, who have shared my irreverence and cynicism and disappointment, ask with utter disbelief, "Who is lecturing whom about what?"

Of course, my excuse for such hubris—my license to preach—is that while developing into a mediocre Catholic I have also, simultaneously, it seems, become a Catholic novelist. Or at least that's what I've been called. To be honest— confessional—the term makes me feel somewhat like the narrator in the O. Henry story "Man About Town." He's an inquisitive young man who spends the day seeking "enlightenment concerning the character known as A Man About Town." He asks a reporter, a bartender, a Salvation Army girl, and finally a critic, whose definition inspires him to spend the rest of the night raking New York "from the Battery to Little Coney Island" to find an authentic Man About Town. As he begins his search, he steps off a curb, is hit by a car, and wakes the next morning in the hospital, where a young doctor shows him the newspaper report of his accident. The article closes with the lines "His injuries were not serious. He appeared to be a typical Man About Town."

In my own attempt to seek enlightenment concerning the character known as The Catholic Novelist, I have time and again come to no more definitive conclusion than that I seem to be one. It strikes me as a rather pallid qualification, for both a preacher and a novelist. If I am sunk a hundred or two hundred pages into a work of fiction, the thought that I am reading a Catholic novel serves as neither lifeline nor anchor— if the novel's good, I float; if it's bad, I don't. Nor would the promise of a "Catholic" novel get me to open a book in the first place.

That my novels have what Flannery O'Connor referred to as a "Catholic decor" is true enough. My characters, for the most part, are Roman Catholics, born Catholic, raised Catholic. Churchgoers, members of a church community, they know the lives of the saints, the niceties of the sacraments, the rules, the rituals. To borrow from O'Connor, that most Catholic of Catholic novelists, they know so thoroughly what they believe that they don't have to think about it.

They believe in the Incarnation, the Trinity, the communion of saints, the resurrection of the body, and life everlasting. Their faith is genetic, cultural, bloodborne, and as such it is cause for neither fanaticism nor zealotry, crisis nor grief. It is, like language itself, a way of ordering the world, expressing emotion, communicating need. It is, forever, their first language.

These Catholics may be the subjects of much of my fiction, but their Catholicism is not. As a fiction writer, I am not interested in conversion, transubstantiation, the mystical body of Christ, the infallibility of the pope, Aquinas, or Augustine. My novels have a "Catholic decor" not because I have anything original to say about Catholicism but because I know it, because it is my first spiritual language as well, and also because—more pertinent—with the religious lives of my characters firmly established, I can try to understand what lies beneath: what is, in some way, pre-religious, the first impulse, the initial yearning, the earliest, embryonic indication of the substance of things hoped for.

I don't write about Catholics because of my own faith, lackluster yet persistent, but because by doing so I hope to discover—percolating up out of all the assurances (authentic or not) that the church, the life of Christ, provides—what it is that sparks the need for faith in the first place.

Time and again I have discovered that for my own characters, at least, that need is founded in a simple, stubborn, unrelenting refusal to be comforted. W. B. Yeats posed the question

But is there any comfort to be found?
Man is in love and loves what vanishes,
What more is there to say?

And Billy, in my novel *Charming Billy,* soaked in both alcohol and the Irish poet himself, paraphrased the question in the language of his faith:

"Death is a terrible thing," Billy said. "Our Lord knew it. Our Lord knew it was terrible. Why would He have shed His own blood if death wasn't terrible?" There was another pause, another sip of whiskey. "You know what makes a mockery of the Crucifixion?" Billy said. "You know what makes it pointless? Anyone saying that death is just an ordinary thing, an ordinary part of life. It happens, you reconcile yourself, you go on. . . . It's a pact with the devil," he said. "To be reconciled. Our Lord spilling His every drop of blood on the cross to show us death is terrible, a terrible injustice, and all the while we're telling ourselves that it's not so bad, after all. You get over it. You get used to it. . . . Life goes on pleasantly enough no matter who dies."

An alcoholic, a pregnant teenager, an aging and ornery Irish woman, a flock of would-be writers, a beautiful girl—all characters in my fictional world who refuse to be reconciled to the death of those they love, to the past that contains such loss, or to the future that will deliver it. Who stand stubbornly against the inevitable, argue vehemently against the irrefutable, remain outraged over the unchangeable, undeniable fact that "man is in love and loves what vanishes." Unacceptable, they cry, these characters of mine, in their cups, in their old age, in the certainty of their youth. The death of the people we love is unacceptable.

I don't claim any originality for them in this. Their stubborn refusal to accept the inevitable is nothing new in literature—

it is, often enough, literature's very reason for being. Two examples come immediately to mind. Here's Edna St. Vincent Millay, in "Dirge Without Music":

> I am not resigned to the shutting away of loving hearts in the hard
>   ground.
> So it is, and so it will be, for so it has been, time out of mind:
> Into the darkness they go, the wise and the lovely. Crowned
> With lilies and with laurel they go; but I am not resigned.

And Federico García Lorca, in "Lament for the Death of a Bullfighter":

> Because your death is forever
> Like everyone else's who ever died on Earth,
> like all dead bodies discarded
> on rubbish heaps with mongrels' corpses.
>
> But no one knows you. No one. But I sing you—
> sing your profile and your grace, for later on.

Outraged, unreasonable, obsessed—as any lunatic, lover, or poet must be—my Catholic characters carry in their blood the promises of their faith, carry on their tongues the tenets of their church, and yet still their spirits rebel against time, against loss, unreconciled, refusing to be resigned.

"I wanted to banish," my lovely teenager says in *Child of My Heart,*

> every parable, every song, every story ever told, even by me, about
> children who never returned. . . . I wanted them scribbled over,
> torn up. Start over again. Draw a world where it simply doesn't
> happen, a world of only color, no form. Out of my head and more

to my liking: a kingdom by the sea, eternal summer, a brush of fairy wings and all dark things banished, age, cruelty, pain, poor dogs, dead cats, harried parents, lonely children, all the coming griefs, all the sentimental, maudlin tales fashioned out of the death of children.

If death is forever, the unwed mother in *That Night* reasons, then love is meaningless.

Faced with the death of those they love, these characters of mine don't seek some vague afterlife. What they seek, what they demand, against all reason, is the return of the loved one in all of his or her familiarity, the profile and the grace, as García Lorca called it, "the answers quick and keen, the honest look" in Millay's poem. My characters, my fictional Catholics, understand the church's promise of eternal life but nevertheless find it lacking. For what they really want is life returned to them, the world returned to them, in all its magnificence and love and heartbreaking detail. Life uncompromised by death, death utterly defeated. Anything less is unacceptable.

It is a mad, unreasonable demand, of course, but it is also, it seems to me, the primitive impulse that makes faith necessary. It is the mad, unreasonable demand—and promise—made by Christ himself.

When Jesus tells Martha, "Your brother will rise," she replies as any one of us pretty-good-to-middling Catholics might, as one well trained in the language of faith should: "I know he will rise," she replies, "in the resurrection on the last day." If ever a false Messiah had an out, here it was. Jesus had only to tell her, *Right you are; you get an A.* What he does instead, mad prophet, is refuse such easy comfort. He becomes, John tells us, troubled, deeply perturbed. He weeps. "See how he loved him," the onlookers say. And then Jesus calls Lazarus from the grave. Jesus restores what has vanished, returns Lazarus to life, to his sisters, returns not the soul or the spirit, the memory or the ghost, but the man himself, the profile and the grace, the honest look, the laughter, the love—and proves to us that death is not forever.

In his refusal to be reconciled, Jesus makes possible our impossible hopes, confirms our own primitive rebellion against that terrible thing that is the death of those we love. And reminds us—or should remind us, if we can just shake ourselves from the numbing familiarity of the tenets of our church, the platitudes, the rote rituals, and the petty obsessions—that ours is a mad, rebellious faith, one that flies in the face of all reason, all evidence, all sensible injunctions to be comforted, to be comfortable. A faith that rejects every timid impulse to accept the fact that life goes on pleasantly enough despite all that vanishes, despite death itself.

What I have to say about being Catholic, then, is simply this: Being Catholic is an act of rebellion. A mad, stubborn, outrageous, nonsensical refusal to be comforted by anything less than the glorious impossibility of the resurrection of the body and life everlasting.

In my fiction, I have linked this crazy faith to difficult characters: an alcoholic, a griping old woman, a sullen teenager, and an amoral one who would remake the world to her own liking. But as we face the church of the twenty-first century, my hope is that we nonfictional Catholics regain the courage to be difficult, rebellious, mad, the courage to refuse to be comforted. That we refuse to be comforted by the familiar, by the way we've always done things (priests in charge, laity ushering, women running bake sales). That we refuse to be comforted by our own self-satisfied eloquence about the dignity of unborn life while political or practical imperatives silence our objections to the destruction of life in the ghetto or in the death chamber. That we refuse to be comforted by our good, prosperous lives, by the careful picking and choosing of what words of Christ we will take to heart.

My hope for the church, for us, is that we recall the adolescent rebellion that seems a part of most of our biographies as Catholics, recall our youthful dissatisfactions and objections (whether we voiced them in Dunkin' Donuts or in our permanent disassociation from the church), and speak them again. Or, if that adolescent rebellion seems too distant to recall, then my hope is that each of us becomes the garrulous drunk in the congregation, the loudmouthed, inappropriate, indiscreet psycho who cries foul over hypocrisy and deception and illogic and cliché, refusing to accept the easy comfort of assurances that the hierarchy will fix itself, that Jesus doesn't want women to be priests, that it is acceptable for Catholics to acquiesce to a politically defensible but morally unjust war.

At the heart of our beliefs, at the heart of our faith, lies the outrageous conviction that love redeems us, Christ redeems us, even from death. Following this wild proposition, this fulfillment of our most primitive yearnings, every other outrageous thing we expect or demand of ourselves and our church—honesty, charity, goodness, forgiveness, peace— surely must begin to seem reasonable, even easy. Every other challenge the twenty-first century brings should seem—even to the likes of us not-so-great Catholics—simple enough: a benefit, no doubt, of the simple grace of being Catholic.

Little Gloria
and the Glory of God

Dominic Grassi

from *Still Called by Name:*
Why I Love Being a Priest

People's lives are filled with pivotal and life-altering moments. As one who ministers to others, I am often called to share in these personal experiences of change. And in a mysterious way, I too am changed.

I experienced this mystery intensely with one family in particular. I was invited into their lives by the eleven-year-old daughter, who called the rectory one day. As we talked, I was impressed by how polite and mature she sounded. She clearly had rehearsed what she needed to say to me in order to get the message right. Her parents were not comfortable speaking English, so she had become the spokesperson for the family. And thus it was left to this child to tell me that her new baby sister was born not only prematurely but also with many other problems. The prognosis was not good. Would I be able to come to the hospital to baptize her? I knew that I shouldn't ask this child more questions than necessary, so I told her to tell her parents that I would be there within ten minutes.

Traffic and a full parking lot at the hospital, however, made me forty-five minutes late. When I entered the hospital, I was sent directly to the neonatal unit. I was stressed and concerned: I did not want to be too late. I immediately recognized the parents. The father attempted a smile, and the mother looked terribly weary. They appeared older than most couples with newborns. Fortunately their English was much better than my Spanish. And their young daughter was there to bridge our gaps.

With sadness in their voices, they told me that their newly born daughter was not expected to live another day. Aside from being born prematurely, she had seriously underdeveloped organs, a damaged heart, and Down syndrome–related complications. There was no chance of survival. But the family was at peace because I had arrived to baptize her.

The compassionate and competent nurses prepped us. We scrubbed down, put on our gowns and masks and gloves. I was given a small sealed bottle of distilled water to use to lessen the threat of infection caused by bacteria. We were told to leave the baby's little knit cap on her head as long as possible to keep her from losing precious body heat. Mother would be the one to hold her baby. I was given only three minutes, the maximum amount of time she could be out of the incubator.

And so we began. The mother, with the first gentle smile I had seen on her face since I had arrived, indicated that she had dreamed of this moment. It was the first time she had been allowed to hold her child. I asked the parents what name they had given their daughter.

"Gloria," the father replied without hesitation. He then explained that she was an angel poised to return to God's glory. He was smiling and crying as he shared these words with us. A moment later, the little child of God, now christened Gloria, was back in the incubator, struggling for each breath. Her sister looked at me hopefully as I was leaving. "Now Gloria really is going to be an angel, isn't she, Father?" I assured her that she already was.

That night Gloria died. There was no wake, no Mass of the Angels. For the family, life goes on. People learn to cope even as they carry their sorrow with them.

A few months later, our parish's seventh and eighth graders participated in confirmation, the sacrament that makes sacred the transition from childhood to young adulthood. It was a warm, uplifting liturgy. I was proud to be the pastor of this group of young people proclaiming their faith before the congregation. The bishop did a good job of taking time with each of the candidates, often asking about his or her chosen confirmation name. When he asked one of the seventh-grade girls what her confirmation name was, she stepped forward and replied proudly, "Gloria." The bishop was stopping at every fourth or fifth child and talking with him or her at more length. I wanted him to hear Gloria's story, so I stopped him and prompted him to talk with her sister further. She told the story of her baby sister, who had lived for only a day.

"My sister is the glory of God," she remarked earnestly, "and a true saint." The bishop told her that she could not have picked a better name. As he confirmed her with the sacred oils, I stood there with tears in my eyes.

At the deathbed of a child, in that most difficult of situations, I was able to encounter a couple's deep faith, a faith so strong that they were able to share it with their other child, whose confirmation name will always remind her of the gift God gave to her and to her family and to me, if only for a brief time.

In my life as a priest, I have learned that sometimes grace comes not from my own efforts to help others find God's love in the difficult situations in life, but from the awesome way people's faith touches me and ends up ministering to me. Now every time I hear the name Gloria or hear the "Gloria" sung, I am reminded of the faith of a family and their angel now in heaven, who is truly the glory of God. And because of that I am able to believe just a little bit more.

There have been many times in my priesthood when the tragedies whirling around me seemed almost too much to bear. Suicide, sudden death, the diagnosis of terminal illness—all these realities lead people to the priest, whom they look to for answers.

But there are no answers. My job is to remind those in grief that it is okay for them to feel what they are feeling. But I also challenge them not to forget or reject the truth that God loves them.

How I am going to communicate this I don't know. I just take a deep breath and pray, asking God to pastor with me so that I can be helpful and healing.

Murder in Palermo

Lawrence Cunningham

from *Commonweal*

September 15, 1993, was Fr. Giuseppe Puglisi's fifty-sixth birthday. The parish priest of San Gaetano in the poor Brancaccio section of Palermo, Sicily, spent the day in a round of pastoral duties. Known to everyone as "Pino," he performed two weddings, sat in at a meeting, had a conference with parents who were to have their babies baptized, and then attended a small birthday celebration in his honor with friends. Returning home at 8:20 PM, he had just gotten out of his car when a man stepped from the shadows, put a gun with a silencer to the priest's head, and shot him to death.

Four years later, the hit man was arrested. A low-level Mafioso, he told the police that Puglisi had seen him approaching and said, "I was expecting you."

For years, Puglisi had been an outspoken critic of the Mafia. He organized groups in his parish to combat them, and he aided those who fought them in other parts of the city. He refused their monies when offered for the traditional feast-day celebrations and would not allow the "men of honor" to march at the head of the religious processions. He instructed young children to hold the Mafia in contempt. When bribes were required to hasten civic improvements, he would denounce those who demanded them, and he railed against their influence on a city government that seemed incapable of providing a middle school or of putting in sewers, although a quarter of Brancaccio's residents had high levels of viral hepatitis.

Born to a working-class family (his father was a shoemaker and his mother a seamstress), Puglisi entered the seminary at age sixteen. Following ordination, he worked in various parishes, including a country parish afflicted by a bloody vendetta. He taught religion in a Palermo high school, an assignment he continued to fill even after he was made a pastor of San Gaetano. When he arrived there in 1990, the parish's eighteenth-century church held only 115 people for a population of 8,000, and its roof was collapsing.

Puglisi well understood that the Mafia was poisonous. It not only sold drugs, fenced stolen goods, and had its hand in the construction industry and politics, but, as Puglisi wrote, it also fostered a mentality that eroded both the civic and social life of Sicily. People were cynical about the political structures of both town and region, and apathy had run deep for generations. Those who made attempts to reform matters were sent a strong message. A small group of householders in Puglisi's parish who organized for social improvement found the doors of their houses torched, and their families were threatened by phone and put on notice that worse things lay in store.

It was the children and young people whom Puglisi most wanted to change. He organized camping trips for classes at the high school, and at San Gaetano he hammered away at the same themes: take responsibility for your life and for society; resist the values of the Mafia; refuse to collaborate in their criminality; say no to contraband goods, to discounted (that is, stolen) motorbikes, and to drugs. He encouraged all to participate in such events as the stations of the cross, made through the streets of Brancaccio, as an alternative to the traditional religious celebrations, largely paid for by local politicos and men of honor (often the same people).

Puglisi's basic intuition was that the ideology of the Mafia was radically pagan and profoundly anti-Christian. His struggle was a kind of exorcism in the name of the gospel. To underscore this conviction, he composed a parody of the Our Father in the Sicilian dialect. It can be found in a wonderful new book on his life by the prominent journalist Francesco Deliziosi, a parishioner and intimate friend of the priest (*Don Puglisi: Vita del prete palermitano ucciso dalla mafia,* Mondadori, 2001). In my translation, it reads: "O godfather to me and my family, you are a man of honor and worth. Your name must be respected. Everyone must obey you. Everyone must do what you say, for this is the law of those who do not wish to die. You give us bread, work; who wrongs you, pays. Do not pardon; it is an infamy. Those who speak are spies. I put my trust in you, godfather. Free me from the police and the law."

When news of Puglisi's death spread, there was a huge outcry. During that particularly violent period, the Mafia had assassinated public persecutors, set off bombs throughout Italy, and left the streets of Palermo stained with blood. The murder of a priest, however, seemed to cross a line. Huge crowds followed his funeral cortege. A year later, when Pope John Paul II visited Catania and Syracuse in Sicily, he referred to Puglisi as a courageous witness to the gospel. In 2000, at a millennial ceremony in Rome's Colosseum honoring the martyrs of the twentieth century, Puglisi was again held up as a witness of faith.

Soon after his death, petitions to open a dossier for Puglisi's eventual canonization were sent to the archbishop of Palermo, Salvatore De Giorgi. That dossier has been completed and forwarded to Rome. Deliziosi, Puglisi's biographer, notes the paradox of a parish priest who died at the hands of Christians who were baptized in the same parish. But the paradox is not novel. The twentieth century gave us many examples (consider El Salvador) of baptized Catholics killing priests, religious sisters, and laypersons, often in the name of an anti-Marxist Christian civilization.

Yet, it may be asked, would not the beatification of Don Pino Puglisi be little more than a futile gesture with no practical impact on the lives of Sicilians? It is true that John Paul II has beatified and canonized with prodigality. It is likewise true that some of those called to the altar during his pontificate have caused us to think again about martyrdom (recall the furor over the case of Edith Stein). A clue to how John Paul II views martyrdom is easily found in his various pronouncements, particularly in the encyclical *Veritatis Splendor.* For John Paul II, when a person stands for truth at the cost of his or her life, that person bears witness to the one who said, "I am the Truth." As the pope understands Don Puglisi, the priest was a courageous witness to the truth of the gospel.

An Italian theologian cited by Deliziosi has said of Oscar Romero, Maximilian Kolbe, and Don Puglisi that they died not *in odium fidei* (because of hatred for the faith), like the ancient martyrs, but *in odium amoris* (because of hatred for love). Perhaps such figures can be understood best as what the Russian Orthodox Church calls "passion bearers," that is, those who die upholding the principle of nonviolence.

The witness of people like Don Puglisi reminds us that martyrdom is not ancient history; it is today's news. When the stained-glass windows of tomorrow's churches are designed, their iconography will include guns with silencers, electroshock instruments, barbed wire, and gas chambers to accompany Lawrence's gridiron, Catherine's wheel, and Sebastian's arrows.

The Church at Risk: Remarks to the Catholic Bishops of the United States

Scott Appleby

from a speech to the United States Conference
of Catholic Bishops

*Editor's note: Appleby's talk was delivered to the national
meeting of the United States Catholic bishops on June 13,
2002, in Dallas, Texas.*

For the past five months I, along with other lay Catholics, have
attempted to speak to you, and occasionally with you, through
the media. I far prefer the present forum, where one's words
cannot be edited to support a preexisting story line with
invisible headlines that read: "New Evidence of Catholic
Church Decadence," "Church Cannot Do Anything Right," or
"See—We Told You So." Certainly in the court of public opinion the church is now guilty until proven otherwise. We

shouldn't be surprised: we live in a culture that permits everything and forgives nothing.

The painful truth, of course, is that the media did not create this scandal; we created it. Indeed, the mainstream media has done the church a service by exposing that which was shrouded in darkness. Only in the light can truth prevail and healing and repentance begin. That the media has focused with such intensity on the scandal is a kind of testimony, odd though it may be, to the fact that American society rightly expects more of the church—more purity, more fidelity to the gospel, more compassion, more holiness. In a way that is not always balanced or fair, and is certainly painful, the people are nonetheless calling the church to purify itself and to be its best self—the image of the compassionate God in the midst of the world.

Did I say *we* created this crisis? I speak only for myself, not for the sixty million–plus laity, many of whom may protest: *We* did not create this scandal! The pedophile priests created it; the bishops who reassigned them, deceiving not only the unsuspecting parishioners but also, incredibly, their fellow pastors and bishops, created it. Surely the laity is innocent and has every right to be outraged.

And of course they are right: the laity did not create this crisis; indeed, some of the laity are the direct victims of the crisis, while many, many others, including the disadvantaged and those most in need of social and pastoral assistance, are threatened with the reduction of services provided by the church as assets get rerouted to cover the legal costs of the abuse.

What did create this crisis? The root of the problem is the lack of accountability on the part of the bishops, which allowed a severe moral failure on the part of some priests and bishops to put the legacy, reputation, and good work of the church in peril. The lack of accountability, in turn, was fostered by a closed clerical culture that infects the priesthood, isolating some priests and bishops from the faithful and from one another.

No one can safely generalize about a group as huge, complex, and amorphous as "the laity." It is also wrong to generalize about you, the bishops. Indeed, many of you are not only blameless in the current scandal, but you have also acted honorably in the incredibly difficult balancing act you are called upon to perform. You did not protect abusive priests, nor have you attempted to circle the wagons or clamp down on lay "dissent" when outraged parishioners and priests in recent months have demanded accountability for episcopal misdeeds. Other bishops, however, have behaved atrociously, angering fellow bishops and priests, whose reputations have been tarnished by those whose actions have been marked by arrogance, lack of repentance, and repeated failure to be collegial and consultative, except in an upward direction.

What's at stake in the present crisis is the viability of the church's moral and pastoral mission in the United States on the scale of its historic legacy; at stake is the reputation of the priesthood; at risk is the moral and pastoral authority of the bishops and the church's credibility on social justice as well as sexual teaching. Whether the Catholic Church as currently governed and managed can proclaim the gospel effectively in this milieu is an open question.

The laity must always be receptive to frank talk from our bishops about our own failings. And in that same spirit of candor, born not of spite but of love for the church and respect for your office, we must reproach you for your attitudes and behavior that have given scandal to the faithful, especially to the young. A good friend of mine, hearing I would be addressing you, sent me the following message:

You and I are the father of teenagers who are experiencing all that teenagers experience. Our children struggle with the whole concept of church, the nature of God, the tradition into which they've been born. I am confident that God will speak to each of them at some point in their lives, perhaps when they are ready to listen. Sooner better than later. But you and I both know that, above all else, teenagers hate hypocrisy. Like Holden Caulfield in The Catcher in the Rye, they will spot a phony from miles away. And right now they are thinking that if this is what is going on with the church, they want no part of it.

When Jesus withdrew temporarily from the crowds and led his apostles to Caesarea Philippi, he posed two questions to them: What are the people saying about me? And who do you say that I am?

Today, after five months of unrelenting revelations of clerical and episcopal misdeeds, one is compelled to ask: What are they saying about you, the successors to the apostles? I don't think the suspense will be broken if we admit that at this particular moment in American history, they are *not* comparing you to Christ and his apostles.

They are saying, rather, that this scandal is only incidentally about the terrible sin and crime of the sexual abuse of minors by a small minority of priests, that the underlying scandal is the behavior and attitudes of the Catholic bishops—not just *then,* ten or fifteen or twenty years ago, when the abusive priests were reassigned, but even *now,* after all the sorry revelations to date! They are saying that the bishops, even now, have not yet engaged the victims in a way that conveys that the church begins to comprehend the profoundly devastating effect of sexual abuse at the hands of a priest, one whose hands also consecrate the Eucharist, baptize the infant, and forgive the sinner. If a bishop had any idea how soul shattering the loss of self-esteem, how deep the wounds of betrayal, the people are saying, he could never have contemplated, even for a moment, putting other children in jeopardy by relinquishing his moral authority to a therapist, or by bowing to the pressure of the pastoral need for active priests, or, what is worse, by being governed by a misguided sense of sympathy for brother priests.

They are saying, most distressingly, that the seminaries and the priesthood have been made vulnerable to the unstable and to the immoral, and that (some of) you bishops are complicit in this development.

They are saying what months ago would have been unthinkable: that the church is not safe for the innocent, the young, the vulnerable—that it is morally bankrupt. Astonishingly, they are saying this of the church whose priests and religious have nurtured the weak, fed the hungry, educated and formed generations of immigrants and their children and grandchildren. They are saying this about the bishops, who have spoken the truth before the political powers of this nation and who continue to testify on behalf of the marginalized, the weak, the unborn, and the other defenseless ones in American society. They are saying this of the priests and women religious and lay ministers who built vast expanses of the social-service infrastructure of this nation and who contributed to some of its most glorious achievements as a democratic society!

They are saying that the failures of the hierarchy extend to your arrogation of unchecked authority over finances and legal strategies, to cover-ups and fiscal malfeasance.

They are saying that some members of the hierarchy, including those at the center of the storm, remain unrepentant and even defiant, blaming the culture, the media, or their ecclesial opponents for the disgrace that has been visited upon them.

They are saying that you are divided among yourselves, and that some of you even take pleasure or comfort in the travails of rival bishops.

I am saddened to report, from our perch here at the Texan equivalent of Caesarea Philippi, that they are saying all of these things. And let us not even consider what our enemies are saying!

And what are your priests saying? Not much; they are reeling, suffering untold pain, and they would be in hiding, shamefaced and feeling abandoned, were it not for some of you and for their parishioners. The people to whom these more than forty thousand priests daily minister, knowing that their priests are good, heroic, and often holy men, refuse to hold them accountable for the egregious sins of the few. In their collective wisdom, the faithful hold priests accountable for their behavior—no more, no less. They want to know if the priest keeps his promises and vows, if he remains celibate whatever his sexual orientation, and if he is kind and filled with the spirit of self-denying love.

On this matter of reassigning predator priests, the apologies issuing from bishops and cardinals will not be heard unless and until they go beyond the rhetoric of "mistakes and errors" and name the protection of abusive priests for what it is—a sin, born of the arrogance of power. The bitter fruit of clericalism is the often un-reflected-upon assumption that by virtue of ordination alone a priest is spiritually and morally superior to the laity.

This is difficult for some of you to hear, and some of you will refuse, even now, to listen to it. But I remind you that a remarkable—and, to my mind, encouraging—development in response to the danger we now face is the fact that Catholics on the right, on the left, and in the "deep middle" are all in basic agreement as to the cause of this scandal: a betrayal of fidelity enabled by the arrogance that comes with unchecked power. Karl Rahner said that one of the most devastating effects of sin is the sinner's inability to recognize his behavior as sinful. Sin's cloaking of its presence occurs whenever a bishop, archbishop, or cardinal assumes quietly that he is accountable to no one but God and the Holy Father—that only he, as successor to the apostles, knows what is best for the church. This is an outrageous assumption, and it is the deepest source of the anger currently being unleashed upon all of you, including, unfairly, those of you who have overcome the temptation to the sin of clericalism in your own ministries.

The role of women in the church is a topic that deserves full and separate consideration, but the marginalization of women, wherever it exists in the church, counts among the most devastating effects of clericalism on the morale and vitality of the people of God. Women are outsiders on two counts, being neither male nor ordained, and so are among the most frequent recipients of the aloofness and disregard that is a sign of clericalism. Given that women religious and laywomen not only helped build the church in this country but have been the primary formers of faith in children from birth to adulthood, we cannot afford to lose credibility on questions of sex and gender. But that credibility has been shattered by the current crisis.

The world wants to know one thing: Faced with this litany of accusations, why would anyone in his right mind want to be a Catholic bishop today?

My concluding remarks proceed upon the assumption that each of you has a compelling answer to that question and is prepared to defend the church and the episcopacy with all your heart and mind and will.

Where is the path out of this disaster? I do not envy you the enormously difficult decisions before you. But allow me to make three general points that I ask you to consider as you deliberate.

First, the crisis is primarily a moral crisis. It is also, now, a pastoral crisis and an institutional crisis, the latter entailing complex financial and legal considerations. These three dimensions of the church's presence in U.S. society are interrelated. Loss of confidence in the moral judgment of some of the priests and bishops places the church in a vulnerable position vis-à-vis the legal system and the civil authorities, who will no longer give the church a wide berth when it comes to the conduct of its "employees."

Second, the church, institutionally, is a unique presence in American history. It is not a public trust in the legal sense, but it clearly has a public face and acts as a public trust in the moral sense. The current crisis has removed any doubt that the church in the United States must understand itself as a national body and act accordingly. This will not diminish but will enhance fidelity to the local and universal church. There is no threat of a Gallican model, one that privileges national over Roman—that is, universal—jurisdiction. But has it ever been clearer to us that what occurs in the church in Boston, New York, or Los Angeles can have immediate repercussions for the church in Iowa, Ohio, or Washington? And yet the crisis has also revealed that the present procedures and structure of the United States Conference of Catholic Bishops (USCCB) are inadequate to address the governance of the church on this level.

It may be helpful if you explain to the nonspecialists—that is, most of us—at least in general terms, the relationship between the Vatican and the USCCB, and between canon law and civil law in this particular case. Rome has been very cautious, to say the least, in granting authority to the national episcopal conferences, and I believe that the laity have or will have difficulty understanding what appears to be a counterproductive level of oversight. Please pardon the question, but it is a natural one: Are you not trusted by the Vatican? It seems incredible to the interested outsider that on matters of faith and morals you would veer one millimeter from orthodoxy.

Those of you who are canon lawyers know the challenge of applying canon law within a specific local and national environment. The state and civil society in, say, Honduras, or Poland, present different challenges to the church than the U.S. government and legal system do. To the extent possible, then, I urge you to formulate the policies that make the most sense for this environment without anticipating how the Vatican might respond. Let Rome be Rome; it will be, in any case.

Thinking and acting nationally as well as locally and universally will enhance the church's effectiveness and thus bolster its authority. Everyone is relieved that a national policy will be deliberated and adopted at this meeting, but will that policy have teeth? Will it be enforceable and enforced? In the current climate it will not be enough to say that no bishop would refuse to implement the new policies. Each bishop must be held directly accountable and his diocese evaluated for compliance on a regular basis.

Third, a new attitude toward lay leadership, supported by new or renewed structures, is necessary.

Although the laity is not to blame in the current crisis, our consciences have not been entirely clear on other matters. A significant portion of Catholics in the pews have been selectively ignoring you, for many years now. Indeed, next month it will be thirty-four years since the events of July 1968. At that fateful moment the majority of American Catholic laity openly disobeyed authoritative church teaching, and the bishops, in turn, failed to persuade the majority of Catholics, including some priests and religious, of the compelling truth of the church's position. The laity practiced artificial birth control, had sex outside of marriage, and endured abortions at about the same rate as other Americans.

The breakdown of Christian community, in short, opened the way to crisis. In the nearly forty years since the Second Vatican Council, despite the council's call for greater participation by the laity in the mission of the church, we allowed some of you to remain aloof from lay concerns and to consolidate all significant decision making in your office, including things unrelated to your teaching office in matters of faith and morals, things either beyond your competence or beyond your ability to judge in a disinterested manner. No one man can responsibly bear all burdens, perform all tasks, act with integrity and excellence as chief pastor and teacher, liturgist, confessor, administrator, financial officer, and supervisor of litigation. Not even a company of men, all cut from the same cloth. (Especially, perhaps, a company of men, all cut from the same cloth.)

Despite the repeated objections of hundreds of Catholic journalists, theologians, and historians, active lay participation, including shared decision making where appropriate, was left, like so much else in the church, to the inclination of the local bishop or pastor. In some places, lay councils and clergy-lay collaboration flourished; elsewhere they languished—much like the recommendations of the National Conference of Catholic Bishops regarding sexual-abuse policy a decade ago. The laity's hope, immediately following the Second Vatican Council, that collegiality would come to characterize moral and theological reflection, pastoral leadership, and administrative decisions at every level of the church, including lay-episcopal relations, diminished as we observed a steady erosion of collegiality within the hierarchy itself.

The postconciliar era, as we all know, has been a particularly tumultuous time for the church in the United States. While parish life remains vital for practicing Catholics, the laity as a national body has experienced fragmentation, confusion, discontent, and infighting as the gap between church and society has widened. Might the same also be said of the priests, the religious, and the bishops?

Indeed, these have been challenging—at times, excruciating—years for those who are called to teach, defend, and celebrate the church's proclamation of God's offer and guarantee, through Jesus Christ, of redemption from sin and death. Nonetheless, the faithful are just that—filled with faith! Yesterday we believed in Christ, today we believe in Christ, and long after the current storm has passed we will continue to believe in Christ, from the depths of our being. We will continue to believe in Christ, and in the church, which has, in and from Christ, the words of eternal life and the model of authentic human flourishing.

Some have called for new canonical structures to facilitate lay involvement in the church; these advocates note, correctly, that current structures such as diocesan pastoral councils representing the laity and presbyterial councils representing priests have in many cases atrophied into uselessness, whether through benign neglect or deliberate suppressions. Such calls should be taken with much more seriousness than they have been taken in the past.

I do not exaggerate by saying that the future of the church in this country depends upon your sharing authority with the laity. I commend to you especially the editorial published in the Summer 2002 issue of *Church* magazine under the title "A Purification Urgently Needed." Alongside the many sound structural reforms he suggests, Monsignor Philip Murnion notes that finance councils, and other kinds of structures, did not prevent scandal, and new structures will not do so either. *But,* he continues, church leadership was too narrowly conceived within those structures, and "participation of the laity must be structured into the basic culture of the church through Vatican norms, bishops' procedures, and ministry formation programs—all three."

Finally, a word about the priests: the victims rightly complain that the bishops seemed more worried about the priests than the victims. But let me speak for the laity directly to the victims of clerical sexual abuse and their families: we grieve with you for the terrible ordeal you have suffered, and we pray that you will give healthy and holy people within the church a chance to work with you respectfully to help heal the wounds as far as this is humanly possible. *And* we also worry about the tens of thousands of priests who have never abused and would never abuse anyone, priests who today are afraid to show any kind of affection, priests who are paralyzed with fear, embarrassment, and grief. We sympathize, too, with these good men, the innocent, the unjustly tainted.

Academics can be obscure; I have tried to avoid that occupational hazard in these remarks. But to restate my argument in the clearest possible terms: the crisis confronting the church today cannot be understood, and thus cannot be adequately addressed, apart from its setting in a wider range of problems that have been growing over the last thirty-four years. At the heart of these problems is the alienation of the hierarchy—and, to a lesser degree, of many of the clergy—from ordinary laywomen and laymen. Some commentators say that the root of this scandal is betrayal of purity and fidelity; others say it is the aloofness of the bishops and the lack of transparency and accountability. They are both right: to be faithful to the church envisioned by the council fathers of the Second Vatican Council, bishops and priests must trust the laity, appropriately share authority with them, and open their financial, legal, and administrative practices and decisions to full visibility. They must give a compelling account of the faith that is within them and address controversial issues directly, in an open and collaborative spirit.

An enormous mistake would be to adopt prudent, courageous, and enforceable policies at this meeting regarding sexual abuse and then think that the work of reform has been accomplished. The principles underlying the policies you will implement on sexual abuse—a return to strict discipline and moral oversight within the priesthood, a new regime of collaboration with laity marked by transparency and accountability, a firm resolve to pray together as a body of bishops and as individuals to root out clericalism in the priesthood and in the seminary—must be extended to all aspects of the life and service of the Catholic Church in the United States. Otherwise, the next scandal will come quickly on the heels of this one.

Christ's promise that he will not allow the forces of hell to prevail against the church is disturbingly relevant today. At such times it is worthwhile to recall the first line of the Second Vatican Council's *Pastoral Constitution on the Church in the Modern World*. As the bishops gazed out upon the modern world with all its deeply troubling trends for people of faith, they proclaimed that "the joys and the hopes, the griefs and the anxieties of the men of this age, especially those who are poor or in any way afflicted, these are the joys and hopes, the griefs and anxieties of the followers of Christ."

The preparatory commission that drafted the document gave it the working title *Luctus et Angor* ("Grief and Anxiety"). One could sympathize, perhaps, with their point of view. But when the bishops gathered in council to consider the document, they gave it the title *Gaudium et Spes* ("Joy and Hope").

In the current crisis, God has given us a second chance to renew the church through the joyful active involvement of all Catholic women and men—not only the priests, bishops, and cardinals—in every dimension of the church's mission on earth. The promise of the Second Vatican Council can yet be realized, if you will lead us in that endeavor. Despite the gathering storm of materialism, hedonism, and a culture of disbelief, the council fathers looked with joy and hope to the future.

They did so in full awareness of their own sinfulness and failures but also in full confidence that the Lord, by his suffering death and rising to new life, has already overcome the world.

Thus the bishops named the document *Gaudium et Spes*. Despite the regrettable failures of the people of God in the years since that hopeful day, I continue to believe that they were right.

God in the Tangled Sheets

Valerie Schultz

from *America*

My marriage is not what saints are made of.

I concluded this after reading Pope John Paul II's homily on the occasion of the first-ever beatification of a married couple, Luigi and Maria Beltrame Quattrocchi. Maria and Luigi, an Italian couple who lived in the early to mid-twentieth century, led holy lives. They attended daily Mass, prayed a nightly rosary, and raised two priests, a consecrated laywoman, and a nun. They devoted their lives to various Catholic organizations. Because the cause for canonization treated the two together, a single miracle attributed to their intercession cleared the way for beatification in October 2001. The prefect of the Congregation for the Causes of Saints considered them together because of "their experience of sanctity, lived together so intimately." In other words, their marriage made it impossible to separate them.

The part that remained off the record is that after giving birth to their children, Maria and Luigi stopped having sex.

On a typical evening at our house, one might observe a table strewn with algebra homework; a basket of unfolded laundry; a frantic search for an important permission slip that is due the next morning (or else); a very full dish rack; cello practice; two dogs who want to play; perhaps a sisterly squabble; and two parents who, though tired, entertain at least a random thought about having sex. Where is the holy in all of that?

May I gently suggest: everywhere?

I don't mean to be snide about the shining example of the Blessed Quattrocchis. Their faith and accomplishments are surely to be emulated. As the pope noted, they "kept the lamp of the faith burning." The pope beatified them on the twentieth anniversary of the apostolic exhortation *Familiaris Consortio,* a document that highlights "the centrality of marriage and the mission of the family." The Quattrocchis as a married couple are a milestone along the path of the communion of saints.

But if marriage is a source of sacramental grace, why are we as a church so uncomfortable about sex?

When two people who choose celibacy as a way of becoming closer to God are beatified as a married couple, the message to us married people is mixed, because we are the ones who are supposed to be having sex! We are allowed and encouraged to have sex. We are the celebration of sex. All of those shoes and backpacks in a pile in my front hall belong to the embodiments of sex. I'm taking a Catholic stand when I say that sex is good.

Of course I am not talking about casual, sporting, movie sex. I'm talking about married sex: user-friendly, loving, unitive, procreative—and also, to be honest, hot, satisfying, and the most fun of all earthly pleasures. Married sex may not always be glamorous and candlelit. But intercourse is the closest one can be to another human being. It is a bond, a sharing, a trust, a deeply intimate human encounter. It is no wonder that the relationship of Christ to the church is modeled on that of a groom and bride: we are to be that connected.

The pope sees the Quattrocchis as "confirmation that the path of holiness lived together as a couple is possible, beautiful, extraordinarily fruitful, and fundamental for the good of the family, the church, and society." As my children say: totally. We married people are on the path of holiness as surely as anyone else who is following the call of a vocation. While I respect the choice the Quattrocchis made on their journey to God, I do not believe postchildren celibacy is necessary for a marriage to become holier. God can also be in the tangled sheets and tangy sweat on skin.

Is this shocking? It should not be. We are designed for this perfect fit. For biblical proof, I offer the glowing embers from the Song of Songs.

Says the bride:

> Let my lover come to his garden
> and eat its choice fruits. (4:16)

Says the bridegroom:

> Your very figure is like a palm tree,
> your breasts are like clusters.
> I said: I will climb the palm tree,
> I will take hold of its branches.
> Now let your breasts be like clusters of the vine
> and the fragrance of your breath like apples,
> And your mouth like an excellent wine. (7:8–10)

The bride and bridegroom sing a delicious, teasing ode to sex, full of juicy and physical imagery, with which any happily married couple would agree. Sex is that good, and we thank God for this gift. Too often we Catholics treat sex as an impediment to the mission of marriage rather than a glorious manifestation and integral piece of that mission. We view sex as a necessary evil, prone to abuse and scandal, rather than a transcendent joy.

The Quattrocchis bore a sadness of which I must make note: they were never grandparents. All four of their children chose lives of celibacy. While I encourage my four daughters in vocational discernment, I'm afraid that if they someday choose childlessness, I will mourn my unborn grandchildren. My father often watches my children at play and then says to me, "It's what makes the world go round." I never tire of hearing him say that: the continuing generations not only spin the globe; they are a gift from heaven too. Perhaps the Quattrocchis' example of celibacy contributed to their children's choices.

I have to hope that when a husband and wife demonstrate physical affection, it too is a positive example of divine intimacy to their children. I must credit my wise and learned friend Dr. Greer Gordon with the reflection that healthy examples of sexuality in the context of marriage are essential to form sexually healthy future adults, which is a painfully lively concern for Catholics right now. Dr. Gordon, speaking at the 2002 Los Angeles Religious Education Congress, challenged married theologians to write about their sacrament and vocation, about what it means to be married and to be in relationship with God. While I claim no theological credentials, I offer this beginning advice: the sublime Song of Songs needs to be lived in the rush and routine of the everyday.

In our house on a typical night, one may not find a rosary in use. But there are bedtime prayers and blessings, hugs and kisses, a spirit of love, the quiet world turning, and maybe even the lovemaking of two searching, aging, journeying married souls. In our house can be found the reach for what is holy—even though there are no resident saints.

Conjugating

Judith Valente

from *Folio*

I was the only public
that September at St. Aloysius

third desk from last
the alphabet outskirts of class

only Barbara Zombrowski
Jane Zaccaro farther asea

My body a stranger
in alien clothes:

pleated skirt, white kneesocks
Peter Pan collar buttoned to the neck

In freshman art
Mrs. Cirone asked us

to observe a sumac
describe what we saw

and some said nature
and others said summer

I said the branches
were the serpent tresses of Medusa

—we had read *Bulfinch's Mythology*
in Sister Helen Jean's Latin class—

the bark the terrible wide
stem of her neck

Mary Smith grimaced, Doris Crawford
then Maureen Jennings snickered

Their laughter spread, washed over
the wastebaskets, George Washington's

portrait, the crucifix above
the blackboard in Room 202

I wanted to run from that place
in my stiff new regulation loafers

from the girls who lived in the stone houses
on Bentley and Fairmont Avenues

who summered at Avon-by-the-Sea
knew by heart the Apostles' Creed

the Joyful, Sorrowful
and Glorious Mysteries

But I knew my mother
at that moment

stood ankle-deep in red rubber boots
in a pool of gray water

hosing down cucumbers
at Wachsberg's Pickle Works

so she could earn $1.05 an hour
squirrel away a few dollars each week

to pay my $600 tuition
and at three o'clock

when Sam Wachsberg blew his plastic whistle
remove the boots, pack up her lunch sack

take home the Broadway bus
smelling of sweet relish, pickled onions

while the schoolkids sniffed
her clothes, laughed behind her back.

I learned how to calculate
the square root of a hundred twenty-seven

memorized the Holy Sonnets
the symbols of the elements

mastered each declension and conjugation:
amo, amas, amat

Ad Majorem Dei Gloriam

James Martin, SJ

from *America*

For some years my mother has lamented—and this is not too strong a word—the fact that I never studied Latin. Whenever she spies a phrase in Latin inscribed on a church facade, or comes across a Latin quote in a book or an article, or hears an unfamiliar Latin hymn during a Mass, and I am unable to translate it properly, she will inevitably sigh. "All that Jesuit training," she'll say sadly, "and you still don't know any Latin. I just can't believe it."

Normally I point out that having entered the Society of Jesus at an advanced age, I hadn't as much time to take up ancient languages as did my forebears, who entered at sixteen or seventeen and had plenty of opportunities for their Cicero and Ovid. Moreover, there are many scholars, Jesuit and otherwise, who know Latin far better than I ever could. Even if I studied for many years, I would not be able to match the accuracy of their translations. So better to rely on them.

Sadly, these explanations fail to satisfy. And when I remind my mother that I do in fact know a few other languages, including a smattering of Greek, and can even translate some of the New Testament, she will frown as if this is clearly beside the point; besides, who ever heard of any Attic Greek songs being sung during Mass?

Lately, though, I have been thinking that perhaps my mother is right after all. I could use some Latin. Not for my work, as she might suspect, but rather for my day-to-day life in Jesuit community. For as it turns out, nearly everyone in my house seems to speak this supposedly dead language.

In the past, Jesuits who entered the order after high school would first complete novitiate and then be sent to the juniorate, a two-year college-level program heavily oriented to the classics. And not only did these "juniors" study Latin per se, but many of their other classes were conducted in Latin as well. You have to admit that this is pretty impressive; geometry, you'll recall, is hard enough in English.

Of course there is still much Latin that endures in the everyday language of American Jesuits, both young and old. First-year novices are still called *secundi*. During weekends in most novitiates one does *manualia*, not housework. One completes *informationes* (personal evaluations) on men preparing to enter another stage of formation. The other night a Jesuit in our house spoke of a meeting with the *formatores*, that is, those responsible for Jesuit formation, and everyone—including me—knew what he was talking about.

But living in my particular community, including as it does so many classically trained seniors, can be daunting. Last month a note went up on the community bulletin board headed by the phrase *Ne auferatur.*

Now I knew it meant *don't* do something, but what? Don't do what? It looked like "Nosferatu," but I figured it was highly unlikely that our superior had posted a note referring to a 1920s German Expressionist horror film.

Finally someone saw me staring at it and said, "Don't remove." Only a few days later another Latin note went up on the board, which said . . . well, I have no idea what it said. So whatever it was asking me to do, I certainly haven't done it.

At the preprandials after Mass there will sometimes be told, believe it or not, Latin jokes consisting of funny things said by long-ago teachers to addled Jesuit students. This is how the jokes sound, at least to me:

"So then the junior asks, '*Quid blah, blah, blah, blah, blah?*'"

"And then the father rector says, '*Quod blah, blah, blah, blah, blah!*'"

"Ha! Ha! Ha!" Uproarious laughter from the older fathers, a pause, and then to me, "Oh, that means . . . "

While much of this is simply confusing, I have discovered that there is an excellent spiritual benefit from my ignorance in this area. It does wonders for my humility. Or, as my mother would undoubtedly prefer, my *humilitas.*

The Grace of Aridity, & Other Comedies

Kathleen Norris

from *Portland Magazine*

It's all about water, and grace.

Our planet is mostly water, as are we. One fact of nature that astonished and delighted me when I first encountered it as a child, and that I still treasure as evidence of the essential unity of all things, is that human blood, chemically speaking, is nearly indistinguishable from seawater. While we live and breathe, we are literally at one with the ocean, and when we die, our bodies become earth. This is not New Age fancy, but science.

We human beings, however, are remarkably adept at ignoring elemental truths; we'd rather place our faith in technology and keep playing with our toys. Every now and then I read of a survey conducted by sociologists in which Americans are asked what they couldn't live without. The answers are always things like microwaves, computers, e-mail, cell phones, and PalmPilots. I am composing this on a laptop, and as I am old enough to remember when the IBM Selectric typewriter was high-tech, I greatly enjoy the convenience a word processor provides. But I also recognize the computer as a mere tool, a convenience rather than a necessity. The stark truth is that our lives are entirely conditional on our access to air and water. In extreme circumstances, we can subsist for weeks without food, but take away our air and water and we quickly die.

There is perhaps something else we humans can't live without; at least the world's religions would have us believe that this is so. Without love, we are told, love of God, love of neighbor, and love of self, we are nothing; we are as good as dead. Scientists who play with the atomic glue that holds our world together have revealed that at the very heart of things is the quark. They are strange little critters, for there is no such thing as one quark, but only three mutually dependent ones. The original three musketeers, one for all and all for one.

Now think of love as a quark: if we believe that God first loves us, then we are called to love God in return, and to love our neighbor, and to love ourselves. But these three loves, like our blood and ocean water, are inextricably connected. We can't have one without the other two, and we can't let any one of the three get out of balance. Loving God, for example, does not mean that we ignore the needs of others. And loving our neighbor means just that, not just loving those we choose to love but loving people we would not have chosen, who happen to come into our lives, into our dorms, apartment buildings, or jobs. Like it or not, how we love these often difficult people reveals how we love God, and ourselves.

Often the love of self is the most difficult for us. That may seem a peculiar thing to say, in the context of our narcissistic culture. But, as with any of the three loves, the key is balance. Think of the person who is never wrong, who harbors an exaggerated and unwarranted self-esteem and lives smugly. Or, contrariwise, the person who is never right and, laboring under an exaggerated and unwarranted self-loathing, lives self-destructively. For both people, their real enemy is a self-absorption that withers love on the vine. Love itself is inexhaustible—God has made sure of that—but we find that it's not easy to love. That's where grace, and the comedy, enters in.

Grace Disguised

It's easy to like the idea of grace. What's not to like? One of its dictionary definitions reads: "Divine love and protection bestowed freely on people." But if grace is so wonderful, why do we have such difficulty recognizing and accepting it? Maybe it's because grace is not gentle, or made-to-order. It often comes disguised as loss, or failure, or unwelcome change. And in the depths of our confusion and anger, we ask: "Where is God? How can this be divine love and protection?" But if an accident, illness, or sudden reversal of fortune forces us to confront our priorities in life and even change them for the better, isn't that grace?

The comedy of grace is that it must so often come to us as loss and failure because if it came as success and gain we wouldn't be grateful. We would, as we are wont to do, take personal credit for what is an unwarranted gift of God. But for grace to be grace, it must take us places we didn't imagine we could go, and give us things we didn't know we needed. As we stumble crazily, blindly, through this strange, new landscape—of drought, of illness, of grief and terrifying change—we slowly come to recognize that God is there with us. In fact, God is enjoying our attention as never before. And maybe that's the point. We have finally dropped the mirror of narcissism and are looking for God. It is a divine comedy.

"The grace of aridity" is a phrase I've borrowed from Graham Greene's tragicomic novel *A Burnt-Out Case,* about a renowned architect whose worldly success—both in his vocation and in his personal life, as a womanizer—has left him cold. He can feel nothing, anymore, except boredom and disgust with himself and with others. The simple pleasure of human laughter has become incomprehensible to him. He finds it an irritation and as offensive as a bad odor.

The story begins as the man is traveling to a remote African leper colony run by a religious order. He seeks "an empty place, where no new building or woman would remind me that there was a time when I was alive, with a vocation and a capacity to love—if it was love." The colony's physician suspects that the man is "a burnt-out case," comparing him to a leper in whom the disease has run its course. He may be cured, and no longer contagious, but his mutilations—in this case, inner mutilations, wounds of the soul—will prevent him from ever feeling at home again in human society. Like the other "burnt-out cases," he will be content to do odd jobs at the clinic if it means he doesn't have to return to the outside world.

The man claims to have lost any capacity for religious faith, which, ironically, only makes some of the priests and brothers at the mission admire his humility. To them he seems a great and successful man who has stooped to help them build a hospital in a lowly, insignificant place. The more the man denies any spiritual motives for himself, the more the others see God at work in him. In one bitingly comic scene—comic because two people are talking at complete cross-purposes, yet both speak truly—a priest says to him, "Don't you see that perhaps you've been given the grace of aridity? Perhaps even now you are walking in the footsteps of St. John of the Cross." The man confesses that the ability to pray deserted him long ago, but the priest (who is half burnt-out himself, and lonely) replies that he senses in him deep "interior prayers, the prayers of silence." As this kitty-wampus conversation ends, each man retreats back into his loneliness: when the priest asks, "You really do understand, don't you?" the man can only respond with "an expression of tired despair."

Aridity as Grace

It's all about grace, and water, and those of us who reside on the American plains know a good deal about how the two go together. Ours is a "next-year country" in which we learn to be grateful even for the bitter pills we're given. Precious moisture may come in the form of destructive hail. A hundred inches of snow that bury pasture grass and make hay for the cattle inaccessible may contain a pitiful amount of moisture. But even dry snow is wet, and that's better than the alternative. Thus we hang on—until next year, when things will be better.

Living in a place that is marginal by the world's standards, and also in terms of climate, can be a constant lesson in grace. Plains people know the grace of living in, and loving, a place the rest of the world considers godforsaken. They enjoy the little things, a pasqueflower asserting itself on a south-facing slope in early spring. They marvel at the magnificence of the sky at dawn and sunset, and sometimes even at noon. They value the silence that can frighten visitors who are accustomed to the noise of cities.

In our environments, as in our lives, the key to maturity is recognizing and accepting what is there. In other words, letting a place be itself. That sounds easy enough, but evidently it is not. Think of newcomers to the American Southwest who moved there because the air was relatively free of the pollen that made it difficult for them to breathe in the East or Midwest. Now we're finding that in bringing so many plants from "back home" and coaxing them to grow in the desert, these refugees brought the pollen, and the health problems, along with them. Think of all the pastureland in the American West, especially land close to cities, that has become suddenly trendy, where fields of sage and scrub and grass are now dotted with absurd mansions. Absurd because they have cathedral ceilings and huge windows in a place where winter temperatures reach thirty-five below zero, and because around each dwelling is a tiny "lawn," its greenness maintained by an assiduous watering that might make sense in Connecticut or Ohio but in Wyoming should be a crime.

Putting this in theological terms, I'd say that such housing developments as we see in the West constitute a denial of grace. As we've been conditioned to see grassland as barren, we attempt to change it into something else. A suburban lawn. We are rejecting the grace we've been given in favor of one we've invented for ourselves. The tragedy is that the short-grass pasture of the American West is a remarkable grace indeed: grasses that look dead to us somehow retain their nutrients over the winter so that they can nourish the cattle or buffalo that graze on them.

In our lives as well, we too often deny the grace we've been given in barren places. When really bad things happen, we tend to blame God or assume that God has abandoned us. "Where was God when this happened?" is a normal and probably necessary response. But sooner or later, we must learn to deal the cards we've been given and look for the grace that is hidden in our loss.

There were grace notes in the unspeakably evil acts of September 11, 2001. No one phoned out of those buildings in hatred or revenge. Instead, the calls and e-mails were an affirmation of life and love: "I love you; take care of yourself," "I love you and the kids. God bless you and good-bye," or, simply, "You've been a good friend." If the hijackers of September 11 inadvertently invited us to the grace of aridity, isn't that comedy? (I am employing the word in its rich and ancient sense, as inextricably linked to tragedy.)

For if the terrorists' intent was to destroy us, they failed miserably. And we succeeded in finding a measure of grace. A more unified country, at least for a time. No riots, no panicked runs on banks. We were a more thoughtful people, if only briefly. We enjoyed the grace of a week without the usual bombardment of advertisements, a week without celebrity trivia. Now that we've gone back to worrying about what Ben Affleck eats for breakfast and what Jennifer Lopez is wearing, or not wearing, we might recall the seriousness to which we were called on September 11 and find something meaningful there.

Death and Life

The comedy of death is that it generally leads us to a better, fuller perspective on life. The prospect of death—whether it is the death of three thousand, or of a family member, or of ourselves—encourages us to set aside the nonessentials that can fill our days and to drop the fantasy that status and celebrity have meaning. Death allows us to live in the real world and provokes us to ask the right questions: What is the purpose of life? What is necessary for a good life?

If, as we are led to believe in our culture, the purpose of life is to consume, and thereby support the economy, shouldn't we pursue wealth as the ultimate value? Shouldn't we, in the words of one computer billionaire, seek to die with more toys than the next guy? Even death might laugh at that one. But if we take seriously the way we were created, with our human blood so like the ocean, shouldn't we also take more seriously our connection with other people, and the planet itself? If the market is our god, such connections don't matter, and it's no tragedy that the vast majority of people on this earth have no access to clean water for drinking and cooking. Water, like anything else, goes to the highest bidder, and those who can't afford it do without.

But is the "right to life" contingent on our ability to pay for decent air, or water, or basic medical care? How much water necessary for human life—water, air, our very gene pool—is truly sacred, and therefore must remain outside the realm of corporate control and the profit motive? What in our economy must be held in public trust for the common good? We are being called on to make decisions about these things as a society, and if we're not careful, we will end up with a bitter comedy that will not be to our liking.

Here's a case in point. Several years ago I read a newspaper article about how the Great Lakes were suffering from both pollution and overuse. In a search for more efficient water management, cities were looking into the privatization of their water utilities. One company aggressively pursued, and came very close to winning, a contract to manage the water supply for a large midwestern city. The company's name was Enron.

It's all about greed, and water.

Driftwood

Mary Vineyard

from *National Catholic Reporter*

Some friends gave me a driftwood crucifix, beautiful in a spare and abstract way. The cross is made of weathered, broken slats from old lobster traps. The corpus is a Y-shaped stick above which is mounted a wooden triangle for a head. Black fishnet makes a crown of thorns.

For two years my spiritual director has been haunting me with the Jesus question.

You know, the "Who is Jesus for you?" question. He is not expecting an answer, for he knows I cannot give one. I accept it like a Zen koan: an invitation to look for what cannot be seen, to stand inside a paradox, to ponder an unsolvable puzzle. When one looks deeply enough into such a question, the mind eventually stills and the heart opens.

So I sit with this driftwood crucifix, breathing in the outlined image of this Jesus who is more than breath to me, more than heartbeat. This Jesus is the ultimate unanswerable question because he is too close to see and too vast to comprehend. He is hidden inside every atom, every particle in the universe. He honors our autonomy, treats us gently, refuses to overpower us. And yet he also appears unbidden, just when we are most in need and have forgotten or been afraid to ask. He stands at the center of everything, holds together all opposites, reconciles all things within himself. Here is Jesus the Good Man as well as Jesus the Cosmic Christ. Here is the one who is as ordinary as bread and as surprising as resurrection. Here is the God who suffers and dies with us and yet is not destroyed. He passes through that which is unbearable and takes us with him to the other side.

I like this crucifix because it is so *local,* springing so naturally from this landscape and culture. In it I can feel the fishermen, the boats, the lobsters, the wind and the waves and the sun. Its substance is soft and worn and faded, as are we who live here, battered by weather and work and poverty and by the intimate, inescapable social exposure of small-town life. Perceiving Jesus in this vague, unglamorous driftwood shape, emerging from and hovering over the absolute particularity of this time and place, requires an act of imagination and will that is perhaps the very essence of faith.

It is the same act of faith, the same effort of imagination that I call upon in looking for Jesus in every person, every circumstance, immediate and local as well as global and universal. So I find him here in the silent, hardworking people in this little fishing village. I find him in their patience and humor and their astonishing capacity to endure tragedy and loss. I find him in all our clumsy but sincere attempts to communicate and cooperate and dream together about how to be a community. I find him in our tiny parish as we struggle to rediscover and perhaps redefine what it means to be Catholic. I find him in conversations with distant friends and in the sorrowful stories of the suffering poor throughout the world. I find him in the victims of the violence and greed that saturate the planet now, and in the heroic tales of living saints and martyrs who are offering their lives to serve and stand with the oppressed.

I don't know who he is, because he won't be tamed or defined, but I choose to believe—and sometimes I can see—that he is here, immersed in the human endeavor, embracing each of our lives, calling and coaxing and dancing us onward. He is here, giving us patience and strength to keep trying to love one another, offering us wisdom, bringing us every day to a new and deeper conversion, inviting us into his infinite life. Humble as driftwood, he moves among us, willing to be the question and waiting for us to become the answer.

The Pond

Ben Birnbaum

from *Image*

Most days, I circle the pond twice. I don't time myself and I've never measured the pathway's length, though I have a fair idea that a circuit is a mile and some decent change. I just walk.

I once read a magazine story about the author William Styron in which he said that he undertook a daily walk along back roads near his home "religiously." Reading that, I realized that I too walk religiously, which is to say, as one would pray: quietly, regularly, steadily—hoping for nothing but to complete the prayer suitably, and hoping for everything.

As I walk in the dark beside the tremoring waters of the pond, a phrase from the Bible sometimes comes to me. It's from Genesis 1, the first chapter of the first book I ever read with serious intent. *V'ruach Elohim m'rachefet al p'nei hamayim* is the way it runs: *And the rushing-spirit of God hovered over the face of the waters.*

Thoreau performed a popular lecture titled "Walking" that was not really about walking but about the superiority of wilderness and about America's West-leaning destiny. The essay that he made from the lecture was posthumously published and is a favorite of tree huggers and interrupters of economics

conferences, but not of mine. Its scorn of farmers and survey-
ors, its distaste for "East" and pavement (even pavement laid
for walkers), and its adoration of lichens and the "red savage"
remind this Jew of what a nation of wood-sprite admirers and
patrons of *Volk* morality can get up to in our time. Still, he
was Thoreau, and he turned out some good lines, including, "In
my walks I would fain return to my senses."

Not that I don't feel the pond's pagan pull. Stepping out
into the sudden sunwarmth on an April morning, I am quite
ready to fall to my knees. So too on February mornings when
the ice cap that covers the pond shudders and groans above
the trapped gods of summer.

But idolatry isn't my game. I may walk religiously, but I
don't go to the pond at dawn to worship. I go to take the
place's benefits and lessons. I go to discharge my obligation
(to self, loved ones, and doctor) to do something about exercise. I go because I have woken many mornings in my grown-
up life feeling that the sheriff is hard on my trail, and I find I
can shake him and his grim posse in a circuit or two of the
pond (and temporarily loosen as well the sticky tendrils of my
unremembered but bloody crime). I go because when geese
cry *oy vey* as they lift their weight into the air, they remind me
of my great-uncles rising from the table. I go because the pond
is perfectly graceful, each of its movements and gestures
inherent and true, and this is worth a man's thought once a
day. I go because Psalms, another book of childhood, speaks of
the righteous man who "shall be like a tree planted by streams
of water, that bringeth forth its fruit in season, and whose leaf
does not wither." I go because once in a soaking cold down-
pour beside the pond I found myself laughing as I imagine a
wise man laughs, and then I came across a young woman
walking toward me, and she was laughing as well. I go because
walking in the dawn, I see dreams and ghosts: John Updike
coming through the mist once (*What should I say ?* I thought),

and Ella Fitzgerald walking with a friend, and Calista Flockhart pounding by in a drizzle and disappearing around a bend, leaving a trail of scent, like fine steam, in her wake.

I have also encountered for brief moments my lost friend Amanda; my oldest boy, who now lives in another city; my favorite sister-in-law, Amy; and my lost stepfather, David, his hair bright and thick again and brushed back like the hair of a man out for a night on the town in the 1940s. I almost turned to ask if he knew all that had happened since he left us.

I go because I once saw a boy of ten or eleven being pushed along the path in an outsized stroller with his arms stretched out and his contorted face raised to heaven in what seemed like joy. I go because melancholy is a sin, and there is no evidence of it at the pond in the morning. I go because the dog wants me to go. I go because I sometimes find fathers and sons walking, and I miss my young sons and my lost fathers. I go because on some mornings I can look at the far bank over the water as I walk and see places I used to walk. I go because I truck in symbols all the day long until I'm sick and tired, and when I see cerulean blue through a hole in the gray clouds over the pond, it's not a symbol of a damned thing. I go because when I was a boy and a young man I woke early every morning to pray in community.

Sometimes at the end of my walk, I put Kate in the car and go back down the hill to the pond, and I stand and let the waters run in front of me until I feel I have just about disappeared.

Holy Orders

Murray Bodo, OFM

from *Landscape of Prayer*

Good Friday, 1948. I am standing on the front step. My muslin chasuble blows in the New Mexico wind. In front of me kneel seven children, boys and girls, Anglos and Mexican Americans. I am inviting them to rise and come forward for the adoration of the cross. I am eleven years old.

Between that histrionic performance—and all the "Masses" I said as a child dressed in vestments my mother made, at a play altar draped in lace curtains with its own tabernacle—and the Mass I offer this morning at Pleasant Street Friary in Cincinnati lies the story of my priesthood.

I look at an old photograph of me playing Mass at a makeshift altar in the rented house on Fifth Street in Gallup, New Mexico. It looks strikingly like the makeshift shrine in my room here.

We are who we were.

Why, I wonder, is offering Mass so vivid a picture for me? Does it have something to do with the theater of it all? In a small New Mexico border town in the early 1940s, the priest at the altar must have seemed so special, so removed from the mundane, blue-collar lives of coal miners and railroad workers. The gold-brocaded vestments alone would have fired an imaginative young boy's dreams. Then there was the respect the priest was given in our Mexican, Spanish, Italian, Croatian world. He was somehow elevated, different, worthy of emulation.

Or is it something magical, mystical? I recall the dizzy feeling of kneeling in the small church of St. Francis of Assisi in Gallup, thinking it was huge because I was little, overcome with the scent of lilies, the swirling incense, the profusion of lights and candles washing the altar cloths whiter, the priest in his gold vestments for Christmas or Easter, his chasuble sewn of spun gold, his shoes polished bright, his hair as white as the alb he wore, starched stiff and proper by the white-wimpled sisters.

The ecstasy of it all—like a young athlete caught up in rhythm, the movement of a Michael Jordan setup and shot, or my father listening on the radio to an announcer doing a blow-by-blow of a Joe Louis boxing match. That identification with the ideal, that sense that you *are* the other. You are Joe DiMaggio or Barry Bonds batting your last homer of the season. You are the priest ascending for the first time the altar of God, caught up in the dynamic of what you admire and love.

Though in some ways generic, the priest's memories of his seminary days and those of his priesthood are unique to him, to the way God prepared him for ministry and the way he has chosen to live out that ministry in the church. The time of my own leaving for the seminary is a photograph of war in Korea, of the McCarthy era just beginning, and of me reading Thomas Merton's *Seven Storey Mountain*. Though I was only fourteen years old, Merton's book held me in thrall. All the places he had seen and where he was born and the Kentucky monastery where he was living seemed like faraway fairy-tale places to a boy growing up in New Mexico, longing to travel, to experience what he'd read about.

So I left Gallup and never batted an eye or thought twice about the distance geographically and emotionally between Gallup and Cincinnati, because that is what you did in those days if you wanted to be a priest—you went to the high school seminary wherever it was. And everyone congratulated you and was proud of you, except maybe your parents, who tried desperately to understand but still thought it was too soon to leave home and were probably right—as parents seem to be in the long run. But I would hear none of that. I was in love with the idea of becoming a priest and wanted to give my life to God.

Thus began my journey from the mountains and desert of my youth to the seminary. I eagerly embraced the rather Prussian regimen of the seminary because it was so perfectly suited to what I was about: becoming a saint by erasing my past, putting on the garments of penance, and embarking, with the earnestness of youth, on the long and arduous journey to the mountain of God.

Asceticism itself became the god I hoped to meet on the mountaintop.

I set out, as spiritual manuals urged, by mortifying my palate: no desserts, no overeating at table, no eating between meals. It is not my rather priggish moderation or even the mortification of the palate that amazes me so much today as the extremes to which I went in trying to be moderate. Somehow from all the pious literature I was reading at the time, I became convinced that if I yielded to even the smallest pleasure of the palate, I would fall into other sins as well.

Such ascetic exaggeration could have made my adolescence a miserable, tortured time. But strangely, it was not. It was filled with the sweetness of spiritual consolation and deep love for Mary, the mother of God. I spent hours before her altar each week, and I lived in a world of incense and stained glass and countless Lives of the Saints that I read avidly, the way teenagers usually read comic books. Spiritual books were the real depository of God for me. They held God, and if only I could enter them, I would enter into God.

But God is not confined to books and the feelings they evoke in us. This a priest must know, and God taught me this in the only way I could learn. It all started when I entered the novitiate and began the retreat prior to donning the habit of St. Francis. I had prayed for this moment, prepared for it, all through the high school seminary years, when most other teenage boys were learning about relating to girls, about living in "the world." From the moment I entered the novitiate in 1955, following graduation from the high school seminary, all consolation ceased, all religious sentiments, all joy, and I was left without the felt presence of the God I thought I carried in my back pocket like the books that made God present to me. In desperation I reached for my faithful books, but God was no longer there.

Then God began the slow process of rebirthing me that I tried so desperately to avoid, to bypass with pious words. I began to experience that dark night of the soul I'd read about and could so glibly assent to intellectually as a way to closer union with God. But now my resistance to this "self-sweat of spirit," as the poet Gerard Manley Hopkins names it, all but drove me mad. I was convinced that I was spiritually arid and psychologically depressed because I had done something sinful, that I hadn't done enough penance, that God was angry with me, and so I increased my penances, unwilling to admit that maybe this was God's work, that God was leading me to a deeper relationship with him in the only way that I would bear. There was nowhere to go, no train leaving for some ideal world, no place to escape from myself. I had to begin anew.

Since nothing I read was any help or gave any comfort or peace, I stopped reading for a while, and the light of my spirit went out. It would take eight slow years to counter the fleet four years of my running from God into a false piety and spirituality that kept the Word from becoming incarnate within me.

A doctrinaire attitude more often than not reveals a repressed personality rather than a person certain of his or her convictions, a self in hiding rather than a self firm in a given faith. I thought, for example, that I was so pure and chaste, and in one sense I was, but for the wrong reasons and certainly not in a healthy way. I was becoming asexual, a pure little mind walking around looking like a man. Like others before me, I was deceived by my own self-anointing. My own mind's "orthodoxy" had led me away from a lived orthodoxy, which is always incarnational, always about men and women.

I did not know it then, but I needed to become a human being before I could become a real disciple of Jesus Christ, the *incarnate* Son of God.

I continued to fulfill the offices of a once-passionate love that I no longer felt. I submitted to the daily routine of the rather monastic *horarium* of college that began immediately after I completed the year of novitiate. I made my temporary vows of poverty, chastity, and obedience and then went on to Duns Scotus College for the four years of undergraduate liberal education.

I feared that I was going nowhere spiritually. I wanted the vows to lead somewhere, prayer to go somewhere, but I saw pride raising its head again, and I, fortunately, listened this time to my spiritual directors rather than passages in books. I surrendered to what seemed an empty routine, I kept what seemed empty vows, and, paradoxically, that surrender led to God's return, just as my mentors had said it would.

In surrendering to the daily routine of Franciscan life, I was embracing the wisdom of centuries of spiritual formation. And since the ministerial priesthood is a way of life as well as a sacrament, I realized I must embrace my whole self and not just a "spiritual" self. In so doing, I was given back redeemed everything I had feared was lost forever.

And it was Francis of Assisi who led me back, just as he had led me away as a boy. Back then I rode the bus out of town as if on a white and gleamed steed to conquer in myself and others the Evil Enemy, just as Francis of Assisi had ridden into battle against Perugia, the neighbor and enemy of Assisi. He rode forth to master and destroy the evil that was coming at him from "out there" somewhere, from outside himself.

Then one day St. Francis met a leper on the road, and he realized that life wasn't about mastering at all but about being mastered, surrendering to God when we meet God on the road. And God may not have the face we imagined, as St. Francis learned when he dismounted his horse and approached the leper standing shamefaced in his path. Francis went up to the leper and embraced him, and Francis's heart was filled with joy. He was no longer afraid. And as he mounted his horse to leave, he turned to wave to the leper, but there was no one there. He realized he'd embraced the Lord himself in embracing the rejected, the marginalized.

And Francis was embracing what he was afraid of in himself, what he had not yet reconciled in his own heart.

Through St. Francis, then, I realized that what God was showing me throughout my boyhood and early youth was that I was my own leper, that I needed to embrace myself and no longer fear the truth that I am a man, not an angel. And that is what I did in heart and mind and soul.

So the reality of the Incarnation became real for me. What I'd known intellectually for years I now felt in my bones, my blood, my heart. God is a flesh-and-blood human being, Jesus Christ, who had a body like mine, whose body is now glorified as mine will be if, like him, I embrace my whole self and love through it, with it. Belief in this transforming truth is, I believe, a sine qua non for the ministerial priest if his life is to be a "sacrament," a sign of the sacrament of holy orders he embodies.

Even my prayer changed. Jesus was now a living, breathing human being whose feet I kissed, with whom I conversed, laughed, and cried. His wounds became emblems of my own previous fear and suspicion of the body that God made holy in his own flesh. The body was not separate from the soul; the body was enfleshed soul.

I stumble in trying to render that insight, that "epiphany" and the implications it had and has for how I live and minister as a priest. I now *am* my body. It is the tangible expression of my soul, my immortal being, just as the tangible, human Jesus *is* the God whose essence and eternal being I cannot see. As Christ Jesus is the sacrament of the living God, so my body is the sacrament of who I really am, an ensouled person created by God to live forever.

I can still feel the bishop's thumb, thick and firm in my palms. The smooth oil, slick with grace. I am surprised at the soft flesh of this man ordaining me a priest—surprised because he spent two and a half years as a prisoner in Japan, a year and a half under house arrest after the Communist takeover in China in 1949, and twenty-eight months in a Chinese Communist jail. He was brought before a firing squad in a mock execution staged for cameras and propaganda, the ruse unknown to him as he stood there in a blast of camera shutters, and him still alive and well, wishing he was with Jesus in paradise. And perhaps he was, from that moment on. How can I, kneeling here in the lull of all this soft sacramentality, even dream of emulating a living martyr–bishop whose pudgy Polish thumb is signing me a priest forever?

That was 1964. I heard him speak twelve years before, when I was a fifteen-year-old seminarian wide open for martyrdom and heroic sanctity—my idealized adolescent contribution to the cold war. His voice, as he sat beneath the proscenium arch of the seminary study hall stage, came, it seemed to me, from deep within his solitary confinement: a single lightbulb, a steady drip of water, and a bucket reeking of feces and urine—the sacraments of his personal crucifixion. He talked of how he worked out mental logarithms to keep sane, that and reciting all the poems he'd memorized as a young seminarian. I chose the poems, fearing logarithms would only ensure madness in me. He kept simple rules for health and happiness: *Talk less, listen more . . . look at TV less, think more . . . ride less, walk more . . . sit less, kneel more . . . rest less, work more . . . self less, others more . . . hate less, love more . . . eat less, live longer.*

But his words of asceticism are eclipsed by the tangible memories of ordination: the anointing with holy chrism, a sign of the special anointing of the Holy Spirit, who makes fruitful the priest's ministry; the presentation of the paten and chalice, the offering of the holy people whom the priest called to present to God; and the essential rite of the sacrament of holy orders—the bishop's imposition of hands on the head of the ordinand and the bishop's specific consecratory prayer asking God for the outpouring of the Holy Spirit's gifts proper to the priestly ministry. And all of this grace mediated through hands that had been tied behind this bishop's back, through eyes that had been blindfolded as he prepared to die for the same Christ whose priestly ministry I was entering.

The Mass is the very center of a priest's life, the Ur-text of all the texts he lives by. He does not write the Mass; the Mass writes him. In the end the priest becomes the text he utters at Mass. His is the body broken, the blood poured out for God's people. The same is true for *all* who offer the Mass with the priest. It is their body broken as well, their blood poured out. The heart of the mystery of the Mass is that each person's offering is subsumed in the eucharistic-bread-and-wine-become-Christ, the perfect offering to God.

The words of St. Francis to his brothers who are priests ring in my ears: "If the Blessed Virgin is so honored, . . . since she carried him in her most holy womb; if the blessed Baptist trembled and did not dare to touch the holy head of God; if the tomb in which he lay for some time is so venerated, how holy, just, and worthy must be the person who touches him with his hands, receives him in his heart and mouth, and offers him to others to be received."

When I played Mass as a child, I was putting on a minidrama that imitated what I saw the priest doing. Now when I offer Mass, I am not just acting; I am presiding at God's reenacting of the whole mystery of salvation—the passion, death, and resurrection of Christ—in the transubstantiating act of bread and wine becoming the body and blood of Christ through the action of the Holy Spirit, who is always the primary actor in the sacraments.

Fifty years after I stood playing priest on the front step of our home, I stand at the altar of St. Francis Church, in Gallup, New Mexico, where I sang my first Mass. They are still here, the Croatian, Italian, Spanish, Mexican, and Native American faces that prayed with me when I was a boy. We are all graying and are a bit slower, and I no longer assume a place above them as I stand before the altar. My back is not turned toward them as I face the altar; we gather together around the altar as we offer this Mass in a shared priesthood that we were made more aware of by the Second Vatican Council. My ministerial priesthood is still radically different from our shared priesthood, but their and my perception of how I exercise that priesthood has changed.

I am still liturgical leader of this gathering we call church, but the emphasis is now on the sacrament of the church itself, not on the priest. Our relating is reciprocal to an extent that was unthinkable in 1948. These faces that were then on the other side of the communion rail and sanctuary now stand in the sanctuary and proclaim the readings of the daily liturgy. They pronounce, "The body of Christ" as they distribute Holy Communion; they take the Holy Eucharist to the sick of the parish. Some are ordained deacons who proclaim the gospel at Mass and preach, who preside over funerals, who assist in the distribution of Holy Communion and in the blessings of marriage.

Pope John Paul II, in his Holy Thursday letter to priests in 1990, said: "The priesthood is not an institution that exists 'alongside' the laity or 'above' it. The priesthood of bishops and priests, as well as the ministry of deacons, is 'for' the laity, and precisely for this reason it possesses a ministerial character, that is to say, one 'of service.'"

I am walking the streets of Assisi one summer evening. I come around a corner and literally run into a little man who smiles and says, to my amazement, "I'm your brother, Francis." I wonder momentarily if I have run into St. Francis himself. In a way I have. His name is Francis, but he is English—from Nottingham—and he is a diocesan priest, neither of which would fit St. Francis. And yet, as I am to learn, his is the spirit of St. Francis pressed down and overflowing.

Years before, he came to Assisi to die, but while praying in the Basilica of St. Francis, he was given to understand that he was to throw away his pills and gather the scraps that fell from the Lord's table. And so, like in the stories of hagiographies, he threw his pills away and waited for further word.

One day, he was walking the piazza in front of the basilica when he saw a young man dejected and forlorn, and he knew, as he had known before while praying in the basilica, that here was the scrap he was somehow to gather. He went up to the boy and said, "I am your brother, Francis. Come with me and I will show you how to pray." And so began the real ministry of Fr. Francis Halprin, he who thought his ministry was over. Several years and thousands of young men later, Fr. Francis found me, like all the others, in Assisi.

He told me of his conversion from successful pastor to a man broken and suffering from an emotional collapse, shunned by everyone but his dog and a prostitute who brought him a meal from time to time. He went from emotional collapse to subsequent physical collapse from cancer and found his way back to Assisi, where, years before, he had come to study the frescoes of Giotto as a struggling artist and young college student. He returned to Assisi to die and ended up caring for the scraps that fell from Christ's table, his "little brothers," as he called them, young men he would take in—for five days at a time—and teach to pray. His daily Mass at the Basilica of St. Francis, his prayers, his "little brothers"—such was his life until he died a few years ago in his eighties. Such is the life of any priest: his Mass, his prayer, his brothers and sisters whom he serves as the Lord himself shows him.

It is Christmas morning. I stand at the altar in the chapel of the cloistered Poor Clare nuns. The altar is oak, beautifully crafted by one of our Franciscan brothers. The chapel and monastery are in the woods of the former high school seminary I attended as a teenager and where I later taught for twelve years. It is a new monastery, founded a few years ago. There are five Poor Clares gathered for Christmas Mass. A small group, a microcosm of the whole church.

Through the ceiling-to-floor windows that take up the entire convex wall of the sanctuary, all of nature seems ready to enter. Deer cross nearby, and squirrels punctuate the silent oak trees.

All of creation is an immense sacrament. All created things are signs of God that we decipher in order to find our way to God. The medieval Franciscan theologian St. Bonaventure puts it this way: "*Verbum Divinum est omnis creatura.*" Every creature is the word of God.

Holy Water

Ann Wroe

from *America*

I have never felt the attachment I should to the daily prayers
of the church. Their depth and meaning have rubbed off with
repetition, to the point where I am stirred by them only when
I say them in a foreign language. Words are tricky that way.

It is very different with my favorite ritual, which is carried
out in silence: the taking of holy water at the door of the
church.

There is, I know, nothing particularly Catholic or even
Christian about this action: the taking of water to sanctify and
purify is a ritual almost as old as humankind. Britain and
Ireland are dotted with springs and wells that have been
sacred successively to Celts, Romans, medieval hermits, and
modern schoolchildren. Some wells and springs are still over-
shadowed by their holy trees—oak, hawthorn, ash, and
yew—on which visitors hang little scraps of cloth, or into
whose bark they press coins in the hope of healing.

Such practices may be dismissed as pagan, but they do not
seem so to me. Water and trees have a deep symbolism to
Christians, too, as instruments of our salvation. That is why I
have sometimes felt moved to make the sign of the cross in the

middle of a wood or at the sight of a solitary tree, and why, coming up on a spring rising by the side of the road or on a hillside, I almost always do so.

Holy-water stoups came very early to Christianity. Stoups of marble, glass, and terra-cotta have been found in the catacombs, and niches and urns for water occur in ancient cemeteries as well as churches. Many holy-water fonts were simple, sometimes no more than seashells; others were grand affairs, proper fountains for ablutions of both hands and feet. A visitor to St. Sophia in sixth-century Constantinople described water "gurgling noisily into the air" from a bronze pipe "with a force that banishes all evils." Medieval stoups were sometimes segregated, with nobles dipping their hands in one and the unwashed dipping theirs in another.

We no longer use the font to wash, but to take water upon entering a church is still a vital act. It recognizes the demarcation between secular and sacred space: we have turned out of the noisy street into God's quiet place, and we acknowledge it. We also remember our baptism, our entry by water into the larger church, but this time we perform the sacrament ourselves, in miniature. And we purify ourselves for spiritual action, even if it is only the action of sitting in silence for a while or looking at the stained glass. I daresay there are prayers to accompany the action, but I myself never say any. The action, in fact, empties my mind of the words that constantly teem there—empties it long enough, perhaps, to prepare me to be silent and listen.

I feel cheated if the stoup is dry when I enter a church. It happens disappointingly often: dust on the fingertips, or a tide line of green mold where life and spirit should be. Whenever this occurs, I find it hard to settle. My prayer itself seems dry, as if water is the medium that makes it work. Our local priest once explained that he could not fill the stoup because he had no water that had been blessed. But I feel that all water is blessed, even six-times-recycled London water from the tap, and I fetched some from the sanctuary to make the point. The action of making the sign of the cross with water is wonderfully strengthening and restoring, no matter how humble its origins, just as a glass of this water, if you are truly thirsty, refreshes the parched body as well as any other.

It also seems important that I do the action for myself. I have always felt a little doubtful about the ritual of asperges. Most priests I know do it with joyful, almost childlike, abandon, but the water falls too haphazardly, as if never meant for me in the first place. There is more benediction in walking through a shower of rain: rain falling softly and evenly on both the just and the unjust, the best metaphor for the mercy of God. Rather than accept the dubious blessing chance throws me, I must deliberately and consciously take up the drops myself. It is a sanctification that links me to every man and woman who has ever felt God through water and thanked him, a line of wordless prayer that goes back almost to the dawn of humankind itself.

The Leper: Robert's Story

Gary Smith, SJ

from *Radical Compassion: Finding Christ in the Heart of the Poor*

Today, with a partner from the Macdonald Center, the social-service outreach facility where I work, I made my first visit to Robert, a sick young man who lives in a hotel in the Old Town section of Portland. His name had been given to us by a health-care professional who thought he might like a visit.

Robert is a frail man of thirty-eight, balding prematurely. In a disarming burst of candor, he admitted to being manic-depressive, homosexual, drug addicted, and HIV positive. His seedy third-floor room was filthy and had a pervasive bad odor, clearly of dead mice, that had me gagging for the first five minutes of our visit.

The walls were covered with posters of heavy-metal performers, some of his drawings, and years of wear and tear. In one corner of the room, where the wall and ceiling joined, a battalion of cockroaches casually gathered around the hot-water pipe, like a herd of little black sheep who could walk upside down. They seemed to be grazing on paint chips from the peeling wall but made periodic excursions down to the food fields of Robert's floor or, in longer forays, to the top of his dilapidated TV (a good place to hide food from the mice). I had never seen roaches move so slowly.

Robert was a little high, and I got the feeling that drugs enabled him to move outside the depressive elements of his life, converse, and relate. He appreciated the opportunity to talk, and after our visit he followed us out into the hallway, where he shook our hands and then gave both of us an embrace.

Alone in a skid row hotel, in a hot, smelly room. Alone, feeling bad about himself. I thought while we were chatting that he must cry a lot; I sensed in him both an off-the-charts interior pain and an enormous reservoir of sensitivity.

June 30, Wednesday

Today was my fourth visit with Robert. He had been drinking beer but had not dropped off into depression. He is slowly revealing the details of his life: years of wandering, sleeping in the streets, sexual promiscuity, several attempted suicides. He now has a crush on me, but it has become clear to him that however suggestive he might be, I simply am not on that planet when it comes to the reasons why I entered his life.

I felt that if we got past all his usual ways of relating to men (flirting, drugs, sex, adios) he might begin to discover the part of his heart that went into hiding when he was a young man. All of his sexual behavior is an entity, disconnected from the heart of the man himself. Some of his behavior leaves me disgusted, and I have to fight through my feelings in order to meet him on a level that communicates care. I know that his behavior is a manifestation of a ruthless sickness that was inflicted on him and that he continues to inflict on himself. It is as though he grew up in a closet and never came out of the darkness.

August 16, Monday

I had not seen Robert for several weeks, partly because he decided he did not want to see me. Then today he showed up at the outreach office and asked if we could connect again. He had just left the hospital after a bout with pneumonia. He is now heading into full-blown AIDS. His immune system has broken down, and opportunistic diseases are ransacking his entire body in the hunt for what is vulnerable. They are busy about their business like the roaches that methodically raid Robert's room for food.

I was glad that he came in; it was clearly an overture to bring me into this part of his journey. His expression was a mix of shyness and fear. But I am seeing glimpses now of his heart.

God, give me the wisdom and courage to be with this man if he chooses to take me along. His pain is my pain.

November 17, Wednesday

Mary Sue and I made it through the cold and rainy streets to see Robert. He was feeling well. He has had some relief from his multiple physical problems, thanks to medication. He has backed off on the cocaine and is no longer involved in the madness of his out-of-control promiscuity. Many of the people from his past have died from AIDS.

Before we left, he suddenly asked if we would pray with him, and so we sat in that crappy little room, hand in hand, Mary Sue and Robert seated on his bed and me in a chair facing them. We lit the place up. It was a positive visit. It is clear that he trusts the two of us.

February 24, Thursday

I saw Robert at Good Samaritan Hospital today. He was out of it, and during my short visit he left his bed three times to dry heave in the bathroom. As usual, he was apologetic for "putting you through this, Fr. Gary." He is losing weight very quickly. He told me that he might consider going to an AIDS hospice after he leaves the hospital. I nodded in approval, but I was thinking that the administrative control necessary in such a place might be more than his independent self could stomach.

We prayed at the end of our visit. He is scared of death, conscious of the shambles that he thinks he has made of his life and of all the people he has injured. Could God ever forgive him? he constantly asks me. The God talk, I realize, has become more and more a part of his vocabulary.

June 20, Monday

Robert gave me a belated birthday gift today: an ocarina, a small musical instrument made of clay that sounds like a Peruvian pipe instrument when it is played. I was surprised; he's partially out of commission because of his disease, yet he was able to track down a gift for me, and a unique one at that. His generosity and appreciation are emerging like a plant from a long-dormant bulb.

He has meningitis, another opportunistic disease, and the virus continues to kill his T cells. He trusts more and more, and I sense that his trust has opened up everyone from the Macdonald Center who visits him regularly—Mary Sue, Mara, Joe, and me. Now we are moving at him with all our wits and prayers.

Be with him, O God. Be his strength.

July 20, Wednesday

Robert has gone to Our House of Portland, an AIDS hospice. He seems happy there and continues to manifest a steady change of attitude. At this very moment I am looking at an advance directive, a document that states that Robert has chosen me to make medical decisions for him when he is unable to make them for himself. This is a humbling experience, and I am moved by the trust that he is investing in me. If he can't make the final choice of life or death, he wants me to make it, just as surely as we all want our family or best friend to be involved in such a decision.

Looking around at the men at Our House, one gets a glimpse of what a terrible disease they are facing. It renders its victims' bodies vulnerable to other diseases and their souls vulnerable to despair. I am glad that Robert is among those who understand him and whom he understands. It is a community. What a strange paradox: Robert is finally part of a community of life, in which inevitable death is the linchpin.

August 8, Monday

Robert left the hospice over the weekend; I was called this morning by a member of the staff. After calling around, I found out that he was drinking and using cocaine again. It will probably destroy his chances of getting back into Our House. I should have figured that this sober period was too swift, too clean, too sure.

August 9, Tuesday

I caught up with Robert today as he was pushing his ripped-off Safeway cart to Esther's Pantry, a hole-in-the-wall that distributes food to people with HIV. It is located in one of the desolate warehouse sections not far from where he lives.

We talked as he rolled his cart back to his hotel. Yes, he did drink heavily on Sunday and slammed some coke. He did not want to talk, was depressed, and had a fuck-it-all attitude. Where now? He mentioned that he was going to see the doctor tomorrow. Given the unhealthy situation he has put himself in, his physical condition will take a turn for the worse. Nevertheless, I did not preach at him or whine about what he had abandoned. I just walked with him down the empty street. I asked him if he would be interested in going to the Oregon coast with me. Good move on my part. He had not been to the beach in years. Yes, he would like to go.

There we were, walking along that obscure street. What strange companions: Robert—short, street educated, gay, drug addicted, sexually promiscuous; and me—tall, university educated, straight, clean, and celibate. We were the apple and the orange, united by the searching love of our mutual Creator.

September 3, Saturday

I drove Robert to the coast in the little Festiva that I have been using. We spent the day at the beach and had lunch at the Nestucca Sanctuary, a Jesuit retreat house on the coast. It was a good day. On arriving at the ocean, Robert must have stood and gazed at it for ten minutes before he could speak. "It is so beautiful, it is so beautiful," he kept repeating, as if he were looking at a new and wondrous color that had just come into existence. He said it had been fifteen years since he had been to the beach.

He could not get enough of the deer that hang around the Nestucca retreat facility. I thought that it would be a good place to take him sometime, for prayer and rest. He kept talking about coming back "to heal."

October 10, Thursday

Yesterday, when Mary Sue and I visited Robert, we caught him in a rampage of suicidal thinking. He had not gone for his radiation treatments and talked instead about another kind of destruction that was not so prolonged. The addict who is depressed is never far from taking himself out. I brought him a sand dollar from the beach, a sea urchin that is rich in Christian resurrection and life symbolism and an item that we had not been able to find on our trip to the beach. He wept over it, saying, "Damn you, you have screwed up my plans."

So he stayed alive one more day, buzzed and happy. I keep asking myself so many questions: *Will he kill himself? What is possible for God here? Can God cure him? Will God? And are such prayers pathetic? I mean, why keep him alive? For more loneliness, more empty sex, more pain, more despair, more mice, more cockroaches traveling across his face at night?*

November 11, Friday

Robert is in the hospital again. This time he has an infection caused by the use of dirty needles. The infection is in his leg and is working its way into his leg muscle. He already has an infection in one arm and apparently couldn't find a receptive vein in the other. So he moved on to the leg. I have known addicts who started shooting dope into their neck veins because all their arm and leg veins were used up.

I visited him today and took him smokes. Out of the serious discussion we had about the fact that he might lose his leg, we drifted into humorous reflections about a mutual acquaintance who had his leg amputated. Robert laughingly described times when he would draw faces on this guy's stump with markers.

February 4, Saturday

Robert's latest trip to the hospital, because of mysterious pains in his abdomen, was ominous in its conclusion: he was sent home amid some speculation that he has lymphoma. Mary Sue and I saw him in his hotel today after he returned. He was a little high on morphine, a drug his doctor has prescribed for him till the end. "Till the end"—now there is a gloomy expression. It is true that they are not doing anything for him except trying to keep him out of pain. If he has cancer, chemotherapy will do nothing but totally deplete any resistance his body may have left.

I noticed Robert's sunken cheekbones for the first time. His is the gaunt face that I have seen on other AIDS patients, a sight that always makes me think of the survivors of the Nazi death camps.

The three of us talked about God's providence and how we have all been brought together. He asked me what *providence* meant. I explained, "It's like when you have some good friends and you would like them to meet each other so that they can grow and love in each other's presence; that is how God looks upon us and tries to enhance our lives."

May 31, Wednesday

Robert continues to waste away. So thin, yet present and gentle and not panicky. He is using less morphine.

Mara and I visited him today. He talked at length about belief and faith and God. "My resistance to God," he said, "has always been rooted in my feelings of being dirty. Like I am always a leper. But I know that we are all lepers to some degree and that in spite of that God still loves us. In fact, Jesus spent a lot of time with lepers, didn't he, Mara?"

He became silent. Then, with a look of peace that I had never seen on him, he said, "Father, can I ask you something?"

"Sure."

"Will you baptize me?"

So there it was, Robert asking to make the move. In many respects he had made the move long ago, but he wanted to formalize it before the end of his life. He knows that he is dying, but what has been a revelation to him is that he is finding himself to be more and more at peace, and that he is loved. And he knows that he is not the author of that peace or that love. We decided to talk about the baptism soon and start the planning.

June 14, Wednesday

Mary Sue and I saw Robert today. He is in that dark room day after day, dying. He asked us questions, and we handled some immediately: yes, he would go to a hospice; yes, we would dispose of his ashes in the ocean. The baptism we will handle when his head is clear.

Then he surprised us with a statement that we will remember all our lives. "I have something to ask of the two of you," he said.

Both of us were thinking, *What now? What terrible unresolved issue does he want us to deal with after he dies?*

He said, "Please continue to go out and be with other people like me, and love those people as you have loved me, and help them find meaning in their lives as you have done with me."

Of course we will, Robert. I placed my hand on his burning brow. It was my best gesture of assurance to a request that humbled me. Ah, such a request. I will call it the Robert Project.

June 28, Wednesday

I baptized Robert today in a simple and modified baptismal liturgy. In attendance were the biggies of his life: Mary Sue, Sr. Kate, Sr. Cathy, Sr. Elsie, a few friends, Mara and Joe (his chosen godparents), his favorite nurse at Good Samaritan Hospital, and assorted others. He came dressed in what he called "cat's ass" clothes, purchased by Sr. Kate, who did a remarkable job, obtaining a pair of pants and a long-sleeved shirt that gave him a distinguished appearance in spite of his gaunt face and emaciated body. I told him he had a disco look.

I used the parable of the Good Samaritan as a Gospel reading. I offered this commentary: "You are the Good Samaritan, Robert, because you have pulled all of us out of the safe trenches of our lives. And your love—so squeezed out of you by life and history—you have claimed again and given back to us a hundredfold. What a grace it is to be present to see you commit your life to the one who is the author of your love. Your faith is healing oil for our wounds."

July 19, Wednesday

Tomorrow Robert will move to Our House. Today was his birthday. I picked up a couple of carnations, abundant in color, and Mary Sue brought him a chocolate milkshake. Though he was a bit groggy from his medication, he managed to chat for a while.

It was a time of gifts. He gave me a belated birthday present, a bluebird in stained glass. He gave us the gift of himself, that mysterious and direct persona that has invaded his life in the past several months.

He told us of the old man upstairs who stutters badly and who, his hand over his shy and quivering mouth, had come to say that he would miss Robert. Robert would have laughed in this fellow's face at one time not too long ago. He was very tired but sensed the pathos of the situation. He said, "Sit down, Gil," and he proceeded to grasp Gil's hand and console him. Robert told us, "However sick I am, this person's grief needed my attention. I told him: 'Listen, Gil, and I'll tell you a story of love you have never heard.'"

It was a haunting experience to leave Robert's room for the last time. As dismal and dreary as that room was, with its ancient odors of stale cigarettes and sick sex, with its discomfiting sights of cockroaches, darting mice, and crumbling posters, the place was sacred for me. In that room, there were no obstacles to the grace of God or to the power of a human being to realize himself.

I saw you struggling in your blood as I was passing, and I said to you as you lay in your blood: Live, and grow like the grass of the fields.
—Ezekiel 16:6–7

July 28, Friday

Robert is slipping. Last night Joe and Mara, great godparents that they are, spent the night with him. I saw him this afternoon. He was pretty out of it, very weak, and so emaciated that I ached. At one point, when he was finished in the bathroom, he asked me to come in to view his body, that bag of bones attached to his spinal column. His body was covered with blotches, caused by the Kaposi's sarcoma. It was as if some crazed tattoo artist had spilled his unconscious onto Robert's body in two tones: milky white and purple.

Later, as he lay there, my hand in his, he said, "Fr. Gary, there are some beautiful dolphins on your left cheek; now they have gone up your nose. Does your nose hurt?" At one point he reached over and touched my shoulder, leaving his hand there, and said to me, "You are an angel."

Who is the angel here? Part of me hates the whole damn thing: his suffering, the premature death that is all around me, the smells and demands and commitment.

God, grant peace to him and to all of us, his family, who are part of his final passion.

July 31, Monday, the feast day of St. Ignatius, founder of the Jesuits

Sr. Kate called me from Our House at two in the morning. Robert's breathing was very labored, and she doubted that he would survive the night. I went out right away.

When I arrived, his respiratory rate was extremely high and the temperature in his extremities had lowered. He was dying.

I am sure he knew I was there; despite his diminished faculties, he could still respond to my touch. And so we held hands, beating back the fear and darkness with love. I asked St. Ignatius to intercede for him and that God might take him this day. "It's enough," I kept whispering to God.

Mara arrived for a brief period in the morning, after Sr. Kate had left. Michael, one of Robert's good friends, also came by. Mara and I left at eight o'clock after I placed a final kiss on Robert's clammy forehead. It would be the last time I would see him alive.

He died at four thirty that afternoon. His godparents, Mara and Joe, were present. To the day I die, I will always understand his death, on that day—July 31, the feast day of St. Ignatius—as a sign for me.

I arrived back at the hospice at seven, after a long meeting with other Portland Jesuits. When I came around the corner on my way to his room, I could see that it was dark. Standing in the hallway were Mary Sue and Sr. Kate. One look and I knew. I asked, "He's gone?" They nodded. I went into his room.

There was Robert, covered with a beautiful AIDS quilt, a rose resting on his breast. I bent over him, pressed my head against his, and whispered, "O Robert, my man, my man, O Robert." And then I knelt at the side of his bed and wept and wept. The paradox is that, in the end, the little guy had been stripped of everything but was surrounded by the dearest of possessions, his friends.

September 1, Friday

Mary Sue, Joe, Mara, Michael, Sr. Kate, and I went to the coast this morning and, after a brief liturgy of prayer and readings, scattered Robert's cremated remains into the Pacific Ocean, as he had requested. The ceremony took place on a stretch of beach where the Nestucca River flows into the Pacific. After we finished, we stood, six across, our arms around one another, silently gazing into the crashing surf, commending Robert's spirit to God. I moved through those emotions connected to him, alternately aware of what a strange and wonderful person-gift he was to me and of that gentle and painful resignation that prevails when someone I have known and loved has died. In such moments, all I can do is fall back on the most fundamental law of my life: God is, God gives, God calls us back to God's heart.

When I returned from the beach, I opened the box that Robert had left me. It contained a few personal papers, a couple of books, and some pottery that he had loved. On top of everything was this note:

My dearest Father Gary,

I cannot adequately put into words what your friendship has meant to me over the past few years. You have been my steady rock in the raging storm. You've been the father to me that I always wished for when I was growing up. You've given so much, and I know you've got so much more to give. Your ministry has just begun. When the time comes to depart this earth, rest assured that you made the difference in many troubled souls' lives. God bless you, Father Gary.

If all goes well, I'll be watching over you.

All my love,
Robert

He has.

Fred Goes Gently into That Good Night

Christopher de Vinck

from *National Catholic Reporter*

During the final illness of D. J. Thomas, his son, Dylan, wrote the famous poem "Do Not Go Gentle into That Good Night." It is this poem that I thought about two days after Fred Rogers died of stomach cancer.

For the past eighteen years, Fred sent me letters every week, called me on the phone every last Saturday of the month, and e-mailed me every day when e-mail entered into our lives.

When I turned fifty, Fred gave me the gold cuff links his father gave him when he turned fifty. This Christmas Fred sent me candlesticks that he bought in Nantucket. I sent him my poems, copies of my new books, pictures of my children, letters about my loneliness and dreams. Fred and I spoke about our wives and children. He'd tell me about seeing the moon during his evening walks, or about a book he was reading. I would tell him about the tree that fell on our neighbor's house, or about my daughter's high school band concert. He would tell me that his son and the grandchildren were coming for pizza.

When I met Fred eighteen years ago in New York, he and I were alone together in the greenroom at the HBO studios for an hour. I was working on a pilot children's television program that never aired, and Fred had come to the studio for an interview.

We shook hands, and then we began to talk about who we were. He told me about his wife, Joanne, and how much he loved her, and he told me about his sons and how much he loved them. Then he took out his wallet and showed me their pictures. I told him about my wife, Roe, and our two children. We laughed a bit. I liked the man. When we said good-bye, Fred suggested that I come to Pittsburgh someday and visit.

A few weeks later, I was invited to do a taping with Fred and the poet May Sarton on Fred's television neighborhood.

We became fast friends, Fred and I, and a few years later, I asked him why.

"Chris, when I first met you, you seemed to like me for me. You didn't want me to endorse anything. You didn't want anything from me. You were interested in my children and in my wife, and you cared about me."

I remember being with Fred at his summer home in Nantucket. He introduced me to his lovely sister, and he brought me to one of his favorite spots, the tip of the island where the dunes were high. We sat on a log and he told me about his father, and how much he loved his father, and how much his father liked this place, this very spot. I told Fred about my father, how much he loved us all, how old he now was, and how much I missed sailing with my father on the wide rivers of Ontario. Then Fred and I went swimming.

After our swim, we sat in the summer chairs on the deck of his little house. Fred worked on the upcoming scripts for his television neighborhood; I worked on the manuscript of one of my books. Suddenly, a seagull flew down from the sky and perched itself on a pillar three feet from where I sat. "Hello," said the seagull, in a very familiar voice. I looked up from my manuscript and smiled. "Hello," I said.

"What ya doing?" asked the seagull.

"I'm working on a new collection of essays."

"You don't look like you're working very hard," the seagull laughed, and then the laugh turned into the laugh of Fred, and I turned to the man who created the voices of those famous little puppets, and we laughed some more and felt just fine.

I lost my best friend on a recent Thursday morning, and when I went to the high school where I work, I heard so many students talking about Mr. Rogers dying. A teacher openly wept in the hall when she heard the news. And then I suddenly remembered that I was not the only one who had lost a friend.

George Washington is considered the father of our country, but for the past thirty-five years, Fred Rogers has been the father of our souls, reminding us that we are likable just the way we are, reminding us that it is such a good feeling to know that we are alive, and reminding us that we are special on the outside and on the inside.

Dylan Thomas was angry that his father died and demanded that we "rage, rage against the dying of the light." Fred reminded me for the past eighteen years to celebrate the birth of light each day.

The poet said that "wise men at their end know dark is right." Fred Rogers reminded us all that light is what is important—and goodness, gentleness, compassion, self-confidence, courage, and love.

At the end of our phone conversations, Fred would often say to me with his sure faith, "Chris, you know who is in charge." This is what Fred Rogers said to us all each day of his life. And we can now say to him in return, "Do, by all means, do go gently into that good night."

Dorothy

Paul Elie

from *The Life You Save May Be Your Own:
An American Pilgrimage*

St. Joseph's House stands where Dorothy Day left it, at 36 East First Street in Manhattan. Maryhouse, the residence for women, is two blocks uptown. Except for the hand-painted signs over the doors, they appear to be tenement buildings like any other, dingy but dignified, encrusted in paint. Inside, the work of the movement continues. The newspaper still publishes a mix of articles about war and peace, hospitality and spirituality, and it still costs a penny a copy, though Catholic Workers can no longer be found selling it on the sidewalks. The house still looks the way it did when Day was in charge, furnished with beat-up chairs and a cast-iron stove out of a Grimm tale. A pot of coffee brews perpetually.

It is the surroundings that have changed. In the years since Day's death the neighborhood where she hoped to build "a new society within the shell of the old" has become one of the more attractive—and expensive—in downtown Manhattan. Art galleries and boutiques have replaced the junk shops and flophouses. One-bedroom apartments rent for several thousand dollars a month. Restaurants on East First Street serve four-dollar coffees and ten-dollar bowls of soup. The new East Village has been shoehorned into the old Lower East Side, and, inevitably, the poor of the neighborhood have been displaced. The Catholic Workers used to serve three hundred meals a day; they now serve half as many, and on Saturday, a day that once drew new volunteers, St. Joseph's House is often closed altogether.

The changes in the neighborhood, together with Day's foresight in purchasing the buildings, present the Catholic Workers at St. Joseph's House with a dilemma. Should they protest and organize in response to gentrification, establish a satellite house in the South Bronx or East New York, or stay where they are as a witness to poverty and plenty? Should they stay or should they go? Although the two buildings are worth several million dollars in the real-estate market, the movement's refusal to sit on principal, amass working capital, or collect interest makes selling them unattractive, and their association with Day has made them sacred spaces, the "motherhouses" of the movement. It is unlikely that they could be sold without a process of "clarification of thought" that might tear the movement apart.

Some of the Catholic Workers have thrown themselves into direct action, leading peaceable campaigns against U.S. intervention in Central America and against the long economic sanctions on Iraq. Early in the war on terrorism, a group of them could be found Saturday mornings in Union Square, site of the movement's first outing, holding up a bedsheet painted with the words *An eye for an eye makes the whole world blind.*

Meanwhile, a religious order in Chicago has called for Day's canonization as a saint. The campaign began shortly after her death. Prayer cards were printed. Articles were published. A Catholic film company produced a movie about her early years, depicting her as "a Mother Teresa with a past."

The Catholic Worker movement reacted possessively. One of Day's granddaughters called the proposal "sick." Catholic Worker communities printed agitated articles in their newspapers. Fr. Daniel Berrigan wrote a letter, declaring that the money spent on canonization should be used to feed and house poor people instead. "Her spirit haunts us in the violated faces of the homeless in New York," he wrote. "Can you imagine her portrait, all gussied up, unfurled from above the high altar of St. Peter's?"

Many can. On the centenary of Day's birth—November 8, 1997—a Catholic Worker's recollections of Day were read into the *Congressional Record* as a tribute. The same week, the archbishop of New York, Cardinal John O'Connor, formally invited the "cause" for Day's canonization. "If anybody in our time can be called a saint, she can," he said.

Most of the Catholic Workers support the canonization process. Those who don't are fearful that the church's saint-making bureaucrats will stress her regret over her abortion, not her opposition to war of any kind; that they will evict her from the underworld of flophouses, rallies, and jails and recast her as the Patron Saint of Soup Kitchens, a kindhearted woman with a touch of anarchism on the side. Thus her sanctity will be wrested from those most committed to emulating it, leaving the Catholic Workers with St. Joseph's House but without their foundress, who will suddenly belong to everybody.

Unexpectedly, the Catholic Worker movement has grown since Day's death, and there are now several thousand Catholic Workers in 150 Houses of Hospitality. Some of the Catholic Workers are fervently Catholic, some grudgingly so, or by casual association. Some see Day as a saint and make a practice of asking, "What would Dorothy do?" Others see her chiefly as a bred-in-the-bone American radical—a pacifist, a woman, a layperson, a journalist, a mother and grandmother—and look to her less as an exemplar than a worthy precursor.

The Catholic Worker House in Houston (among others) combines the two, showing hospitality to illegal aliens on the one hand and publishing long-out-of-print "resources of the Catholic Worker" on the other.

Beyond the Catholic Worker, many people follow Day's example improvisationally. A laywoman ministers to prostitutes, helping them reorient their lives. An activist attorney files lawsuits opposing predatory lending practices in poor neighborhoods. In parochial schools and Catholic Charities offices, older women keep her spirit alive at their desks. The members of a New York volunteer group, in a litany to the "saints of our city," pray for her intercession.

Now as ever, Dorothy Day is a person who inspires imitation, who makes others want to live the way she did. Many have changed their lives at her prompting. She, however, saw her own life as an imitation of Christ and liked to say that the saint is a person whose life would not make sense if God did not exist. Something is lost when she is merely venerated, whether by Catholic Workers or by the sponsors of her sainthood. She meant for her life to point beyond herself—to God and to the poor people among us, to ourselves and to the wider world, which alike always need reforming.

Churchgoing: From Chicago to Santa Pudenziana

Diane Filbin

from *Commonweal*

My father taught me to love churches. A surprising feat, really, since he spent most of his time in bed. At least that is how I will always remember him. He worked at a night job for more than forty years and seemed to lengthen his time away from home by using public transportation. At points in the daytime he would appear downstairs at the dining room table to visit with my mother and to talk with any of his seven children who might happen to be home. He rarely went into the living room, just ran up and down the stairs from bed to table and then back to bed again.

People tiptoeing in and out of the bedroom prevented him from ever really sleeping, so he settled for a lifetime of resting. He could tell which one of his children was home by which artiste was being played, and once, in the early 1970s, he confided to me that he would lose his mind if he heard "American Pie" one more time. That he rarely complained about any of this enshrined him for me as a model of patience, which he held highest among virtues.

He read in bed. I can still see him turning over on his elbow to show me *The Diary of a Country Priest. A Sentimental Education* impressed him, as did other French novels, though he never went into detail when telling me why. He would stack his books on the floor next to his side of the bed until he had thought them through; then he would move them onto his bookshelves. I thought of him as the Proust of our city block, resting but thinking.

He died right after he retired, so he never had a chance to reverse his schedule and start getting a good night's sleep. When I walked in procession past him, lying down for the last time, I slipped him his paperback of James Joyce. I had taken it from his bookshelf, instead of picking up the volume on Christian tradition by Jaroslav Pelikan that lay on the floor next to his bed. Although he was probably still thinking that one through, I chose the Joyce. It was smaller, and "The Dead" was his favorite story.

Earlier that week, on the evening that turned out to be the one before he died, I had left my mother, sisters, and brothers at the intensive care unit so that I could get something to eat and go home. On the way, I stopped at a video store to look for a film that I had been thinking about all that day, Otto Preminger's *The Cardinal*.

I was in seventh grade in the mid-1960s when my best friend and I went to see it. Even then I knew it was a cheesy movie, but some of the scenes have stayed with me all my life. Preminger, fascinated by the church, picks up on themes of pre–Vatican II Catholicism. There is a great deal of talk about abortion, celibacy, obedience, worldly vanity, parish fund-raising, and even the pope's deeply ingrained suspicion of Americans. All of it reminds me of the hours I spent as a girl discussing such issues with my father. The two of us puzzling it out together: *Is the Catholic Church the only true church?* We were so earnest. That was a mark of the time. Watching the movie brought it all back to me. Then, a few years later, a vacation day evoked his legacy even more.

The winter of 1998 had been a sad one for me in several respects, and I comforted myself by booking a trip to Rome in late March. In particular, I wanted to visit the ancient churches of Santa Prassede and Santa Pudenziana. I had visited them before and hoped that seeing them again would give me the boost I needed. For me there is no surer way to sense God's protection and love than to enter a church and see what's beautiful there.

People say that they feel God's love when they are in natural settings, but when I think of nature, I just hope that the basement isn't flooding. I intend to relax someday and quiet myself with nature, but I really am less drawn to a mountain brook than to, say, the Baroque frenzy of Ignatius Loyola's tomb. Perhaps my workaday urban background has conditioned me this way, but leaving one interesting city to visit another is usually what vacation means to me.

I entered Santa Prassede. Do people think of St. Paul as easygoing and friendly? I hadn't until I saw him pictured in mosaic on the great apse, his arm around Prassede, looking calm and relaxed. She is wearing beautiful earrings for her presentation in heaven. The opposite side of the mosaic shows her sister, Pudenziana, with St. Peter's arm around her shoulder. She looks purposeful and his gaze is steady. Christ is in the center, surrounded by his friends, these early Christians. The arches above depict the Paschal Lamb with the angels and saints. Beneath a palm tree at the far left is St. Paschal, wearing nice shoes and the square halo of the living. He commissioned the church in the ninth century, and I enjoy thinking of him studying the plans and nodding his approval of this golden panorama.

I moved on to Santa Pudenziana, just across the Via Cavour. Low, like many early Roman gathering places, Santa Pudenziana invites a quiet approach. Built around 400, on one of the earliest sites of Christian worship in the city, it is small and dark. In the mosaic inside, Christ sits on a throne, holding some papers, and the heavenly Jerusalem is behind him. Although his business is serious, he looks kind and at ease. I had read that this mosaic is pre-Byzantine and free of stylized influences, but its direct effect unsettled me.

Emerging from a damp church into Roman sunshine may be one of life's most invigorating delights. I walked for more than an hour trying to find the inviting trattoria I had spotted the day before, but by the time I found it and realized it was closed on Mondays, the bright promise of lunch had begun to fade. I had but one option. I turned the corner into Piazza Navona, took an outside table at Tre Scalini, and splurged. It was a dazzling finish to a wonderful morning.

As I rose to leave, I decided to visit San Luigi dei Francesi, the French church nearby. Although I had passed it many times on previous trips, I had never gone inside. Of course, people who know Rome understand that the city takes its time to beckon. So, for the third time that day, I left the sunshine behind and entered relative darkness. The church was crowded with workmen and noisy tourists. I stepped around them, made my way toward the main altar, and turned left into a chapel. And there it was, a surprise to me. I had no idea. Despite the poor lighting and the wall of scaffolding in front of it, the great painting's power was undiminished.

There are more important works of art than Caravaggio's *The Calling of Saint Matthew,* but we don't need reasons for having favorites. The tax collector sits at the money table with his cronies. A boy at the head of the table is armed. Entering from the right are two figures in shabby clothing. St. Peter gestures to the boy to wait. Christ, his face in partial darkness, looks across the room at Matthew and points to him. The verb *looks* is inadequate, and *points* is wrong, too, but this is how the action begins. Perhaps the light is more important than the gesture—books have probably been written about it—but certainly it is what makes the painting so wonderful. The action centers on Matthew. This is his moment, his life now changed forever.

Visiting the church on impulse and seeing the painting in the flesh transfixed me. Yet all the while I kept thinking, *If only the boys were here with me . . .* Would my two sons have enjoyed discovering the painting in San Luigi? Probably. But they would have teased me about it: church after church. Looking back now I have to admire their patience. I saved for years to take them to Chartres, but what they remember is stopping at a Paris carnival and eating all the croissants the next morning. What I remember is two little boys in shorts entering the cathedral and, well, looking up.

Several years before that day in Rome, at the time of my father's unexpected death, my family kept vigil at the hospital during his ten days in a coma. His sister, my beloved aunt, did her best to comfort us. At one point she stood with me at a window. "He was crazy about you," she said. "Of course, you were the oldest and he was just a kid when you were born. On his days off, when you were a baby, he would put you in his car and drive you all around Chicago. We teased him about it, because do you know where he took you? To churches! To St. Vincent's, or to Our Lady of Sorrows . . . everywhere. We used to laugh about it. 'She isn't even walking yet!' we told him. But Patrick would say that he wanted to show you what's beautiful."

He had never mentioned any of this to me. He had probably forgotten it, and he certainly wasn't one for looking back. At the time of these visits he would have been about twenty-four and already settled into the job that he would hold for the rest of his life. I don't know if his visits with me as an infant in his arms had anything to do with the feeling of peace and the love of God that I can often summon just by walking into a beautiful church. But I suspect that they had everything to do with it. And for that, I owe him a debt that can never be repaid.

Why?

Andrew Greeley

from *America*

Hilaire Belloc, an English Catholic writer of the first half of the last century, once remarked apropos of Catholic leadership that any organization whose leadership was guilty of such knavish imbecility must have the special protection of God. As we ride the turbulent waves of the latest reprise of the sexual-abuse scandal, we must wonder why. Why did some of our leaders fall victim to the current tide of knavish imbecility?

Some "experts" point to celibate clerical culture as an explanation, with no evidence to support such an argument and no explanation why police, physicians, and sometimes even academics similarly protect their own. So do many church leaders of other denominations, though not with so much dedicated imbecility.

Some gay-bashers blame the church for ordaining gay men in recent years. But most of the cases that have surfaced are of men who were ordained long before the alleged increase in gay ordinations.

The answer, I think, has nothing to do with celibacy or homosexuality and much to do with the propensity of men to stand behind their own kind, especially when they perceive them to be under attack. Under such circumstances, loyalty inclines men to circle the wagons, deny the truth of the charges (however patent they may be to others), and demonize the attackers. A form of groupthink takes over. They rally round to support those under assault.

Clerical culture is different from similar cultures in that the bishop is under pressure to exercise paternal care of the priest in trouble. The bishop, like other priests, finds himself inclined to denials and demonizations: maybe the charges are not true, maybe the so-called victims brought it on themselves, maybe they're just interested in money, maybe the priest deserves another chance. The police have not brought charges; the doctors offer ambiguous advice; the lawyers think they can fend off a suit. The media thus far have left these events alone. The priest vigorously denies that he ever touched the alleged victim. Just one more chance, he asks.

Many bishops, perhaps a majority of them, even the most churlish, feel a compulsion to be kind to the priest in trouble. (There but for the grace of God.) So they beat up on the victims and their families and send the man off to an institution, and then, hoping he's cured, they send him back to a parish.

Should a trial materialize, the bishops—trapped between adversarial lawyers ("The victims and their families are the enemy") and their own doubts about the guilt of the priest ("He still denies it")—are willing (as was then-bishop Edward Egan in Bridgeport) to argue through lawyers that priests do not work for the church but are independent contractors. Or they argue, as Cardinal Anthony Bevilacqua did through his lawyers in Philadelphia, that the victim's parents are legally responsible because they did not warn their child of the dangers.

This is the slippery slope that begins with loyalty to a fellow priest, doubt about guilt, and paternalist duty to be kind and ends either with reassignment or hardball litigation. Moreover, at every step of the way, the bishop's advisers encourage him to give the priest another chance or to fight back. The kind of men who are made bishops today find it difficult simply to dump a fellow priest, and, similarly, their advisers find it difficult to suggest doing so (though in Boston, Bishop John Michael D'Arcy did indeed give such advice).

This narrative might suggest some sympathy for the decisions many bishops made. But I am attempting to understand and explain, not to defend. The decisions made across the country are manifestations of knavish imbecility. Yet I can understand how men could have come to make them.

Mistakes were perhaps understandable before 1986, when at their meeting at St. John's Abbey the bishops heard for the first time a systematic presentation about child abuse. Mistakes became less understandable after 1993, when the hierarchy put together a perfectly reasonable set of guidelines (which were systematically ignored) and when Cardinal Joseph Bernardin distributed copies of his policies in Chicago to every bishop in the country.

I remember harassing the cardinal about the abuses in Chicago. "What should I do?" he asked.

"Get rid of them all," I said.

"That's exactly what we're doing," he said.

"And set up a review board on which the majority are not priests."

He did that too, though I claim no credit for it.

Yet I reflect on how hard it must have been for Joseph Bernardin, the kindest and gentlest of men, to remove more than twenty priests from active ministry. The Chicago system does not work perfectly; no system could. But it works better than anything that seems to have functioned for the last ten years in the Northeast. As far as I am concerned, the statute of limitations on knavish imbecility ended in 1992. That bishops could reassign abusive priests after the early nineties was, I'm sorry to have to say it, sinful.

There were three sins. First, they besmirched the office of bishop and seriously weakened its credibility. Second, they scandalized the Catholic laity, perhaps the worst scandal in the history of our republic.

But their gravest sin was not considering the victims, not even talking to the victims and their families, blinding themselves to the terrible wreckage that sexual abuse causes in human lives. Bishops worried about their priests; they did not worry about the victims. They did not seem to understand that at the same time they were trying to inhibit sexual satisfaction in the marital bed, they were facilitating sexual satisfaction for abusive priests.

When I argue that many of our leaders have sinned, I am not judging the state of their conscience. I do not have the gift of *scrutatio cordium*. I will leave it to God to judge their moral responsibility. I am merely saying that by cooperating with sexual abuse of children and adolescent boys they were objectively sinning—and it is hard to see how they can claim invincible ignorance. They were, in fact, according to the strict canons of the old moral theology, necessary cooperators in evil and objectively as responsible for the evil as those who actually did it.

Yet they still blame the media and the tort lawyers for their problems, as if the *Boston Globe* and money-hungry lawyers sent priests with twisted psyches back into the parishes where they could rape kids.

Cardinal Law argues bad records. In the *Wall Street Journal,* Philip Lawler, his onetime editor, blames the cardinal but links the cardinal's mistakes to parish priests' not enforcing the prohibition on birth control.

Gimme a break!

Denial among bishops continues, now no longer about the guilt of their priests but about their own sinfulness. Moreover, the denial persists not only among bishops but also among priests, who complain about how they are suffering because of the scandal. If the pathetic letters emerging from the office of the National Federation of Priests' Councils are any indication of the sentiment of the ordinary priest, self-pity is more important than the consideration of their own personal responsibility for not reporting abuse about which they knew.

Reparation has not even begun. Until that happens, the reestablishment of even a semblance of hierarchy credibility cannot begin.

As the late bishop William E. McManus argued back in the last turn of the abuse cycle, the bishops must do public penance. They didn't then. If they do it now, it would have to be much more impressive than just a collective service in some cathedral. Those bishops who have become notorious and public sinners must admit their guilt and undertake personal penance.

Resign? I doubt that the Vatican, which does not seem to have a clue about the current crisis in the United States, would accept resignations. (Besides, better the devil you know than the devil you don't know.) It would be much better if the offending bishops would go off to a monastery for a long period of prayer, reflection, and fasting. This kind of gesture might just possibly calm some of the stormy waves. They wouldn't necessarily have to don sackcloth and ashes, though there is something to be said for that ancient custom.

Will something like that happen? Again I say, gimme a break! Cardinals don't have to admit that they have sinned. Much less do they have to engage in public contrition.

In the Dark

Patrick Hannon, CSC

from *Hidden Presence: Twelve Blessings That Transformed Sorrow or Loss*

The first thing you should know about me is that I never wanted to move to the Midwest.

Seven weeks into my first year at Notre Dame High School in Niles, a suburb just outside of Chicago, I'm sitting at a table on an unusually cold October evening talking with the mother of one of my students, and she is asking me where I came from. When I tell her California, she looks at me quizzically— you know, with the horrified gawking usually reserved for sideshow exhibits in traveling carnivals.

"Why in God's name would you want to travel from California to Chicago?" she asks in all sincerity.

Why indeed? But I tell her what I want to believe: I love a new challenge. I heard Chicago is a great town. I wanted to get into teaching.

I go on and on, but the honest-to-God truth is that it was a vow of obedience—the quiet sibling of those sacred vows members of religious communities make—that got me here. It was obedience and obedience alone. As I said, the first thing you need to know about me for the purpose of this story is that I never wanted to move to the Midwest.

My students—all male—think celibacy must be the toughest vow to embrace, and given their hormonal state of being, I don't blame them. Or sometimes they figure it must be the vow of poverty, given their own lifestyles and aspirations. (How do you *live* on three hundred bucks a month, Father?) But I promise you that it is really and truly the vow of obedience that has kept me up nights, sweating and rethinking the trajectory of my life, and made me humbler than I ever wanted to be.

I suspect I am not unlike most everyone else in this regard, especially spouses and parents. Stitched into married life is a kind of obedience that requires great sacrifice too. Both theologically and practically speaking, obedience means our lives are never truly our own. Parents and spouses live that truth out every day, and so do vowed religious men and women.

So it happened that five years ago I packed all of my belongings into cardboard boxes and made the trek from San Francisco to Chicago to begin a new ministry in a new town with a group of Holy Cross priests I did not know. I was thirty-nine years old—a novice and a middle-ager living two thousand miles away from my nearest kin. I told my family and friends that this would be a three-year gig, and with my provincial superior's blessing, and God willing, I would return, like the prodigal son, to bask once again in the warmth of familial love and West Coast sun.

The second thing you need to know about me is that I'm Irish. There is a strain of us called "I'm never truly happy unless I'm sad" Irish. Depression runs in my family, and all of my brothers and sisters and I agree it is because of the Celtic blood that courses through our veins. The Irish writer Edna O'Brien put it this way: "When anyone asks me about the Irish character, I say look at the trees. Maimed, stark and mis-shapen, but ferociously tenacious." We're the kind of Irish who are genuinely cheerful on the outside. We exhibit a spirit that betrays a gritty determination to endure, but on the inside, well, there sits the sad poet.

Now, our *particular* strand of Irish, namely, the Hannon clan, finds its greatest joy in pleasing others. Growing up, we were the ones you wanted to invite to your parties or enlist for some huge project. We were the best lab partners in chemistry class. We lived to make other people happy. The greatest sin any one of us could commit was the sin of disappointing someone else. (Though we only occasionally practiced such generosity among one another, the rest of the world loved us Hannon kids.)

These two dominant traits—the propensity toward melancholy and the desire to please—finally came home to roost for me seven weeks into my stint at Notre Dame High School.

I had moved because I was asked to, because I wanted to believe that I was a team player, because I wanted to be an obedient son (read: please my superiors). But, unbeknownst to almost everyone at the school—my colleagues, my students, and most of my Holy Cross confreres—I was being sucked deeper and deeper into an unfamiliar darkness, a darkness I began to fear would swallow me whole.

My depression was like waking up on a different planet. I distinctly remember walking one morning in early August along the breezeway that connects the school with the priests' residence. It was the first day of classes, and I had a growing feeling of apprehension and uncertainty that I had never before experienced. At first I dismissed it as first-day jitters. After all, it had been nine years since I had taught full-time. If I hadn't been nervous, I would have been worried! (How's that for Irish optimism?)

But somehow I knew that this was more than nervousness. Much the way one senses with the first scratch in the throat that it's more than a cold, I knew that I was dealing with something far more serious than stage fright. Yet the farthest point on my new horizon bore only the faintest hint of the brewing storm.

I walked into my first-period class, British literature with seniors, completely out of my element. I was standing before what appeared to be the entire offensive and defensive lines of the varsity football team, twenty-eight young men who carried themselves with a Chicago swagger and spoke with a kind of street-smart cockiness that had me pining immediately for those old ladies who kept me knee-deep in devotion and chocolate chip cookies at the parish I had left behind.

I made it through that first day—barely—and collapsed in a chair in my bedroom that afternoon. I slept through dinner. It was the beginning of my first—but not my last—episode of major depression.

My students were (and are) amazing human beings. After a few short weeks, I got used to the all-male environment of Notre Dame. In many respects it is like a tight-knit family, a fraternity of brothers. It amazes me still to witness the kind of fierce loyalty and pride such a learning environment engenders in the hearts of young men. In my first weeks in the teaching saddle, the Dons of Notre Dame (a Don is a gentleman) coaxed the best out of me.

Beowulf, Blake, Shakespeare, Shelley: I was determined to shape my students' minds and hearts with these tools of prose and verse. Knowing how much I loved literature and writing, they mostly went along, feigning disinterest but secretly hoping I would inspire them.

But even as I summoned my will and energy every morning to teach, I was beginning to die a little each day. The seeping sadness took over my sleep first. I began waking up in the middle of the night and lying awake in bed until together my alarm clock and I welcomed the dawn. It took every ounce of energy to get out of bed. I would sit through Morning Prayer with my Holy Cross community, finding many of the psalms to be bemusing at best, cruelly ironic at worst. "Save me, God," Psalm 69 begins,

> for the waters have reached my
>> neck.
> I have sunk into the mire of the deep,
>> where there is no foothold. . . .
> I am weary with crying out.

And Psalm 63:

> O God, you are my God—
>> for you I long!
> For you my body yearns;
>> for you my soul thirsts,
> Like a land parched, lifeless,
>> and without water.

Only later would I come to appreciate that the gnawing pain of anguish I felt those mornings was prayer. And though it seemed as if God had turned a deaf ear to my constant pleas, in retrospect, God was there with me, sharing my suffering, making it his own.

By the time I arrived in my classroom each morning, I was usually fine. I thoroughly enjoyed the respite that my workload provided me: teaching, counseling, moderating a club. I actually did a phenomenal job of hiding the truth, and I'm glad I did. My students needed me to be their teacher, and they needed me to be at my best. Whatever personal trials I was enduring were kept secret.

I recall later that semester one of my seniors asking me with well-honed skepticism how it was possible for me to be so happy and positive all the time. Telling him the truth—that even getting dressed was a decision I made each day and that the decision caused me great pain—brought me secret satisfaction as well. Inside I was like the Irish tree: maimed, misshapen. But outside I was still able to be "ferociously tenacious."

My depression really came down to a lack of trust. I was having a very difficult time accepting the possibility that it was God's will for me to be in Illinois, teaching English to a bunch of boys I didn't know. It made absolutely no sense that I should be exiled so far away from family and friends, from anything that was familiar to me. I was deeply lonely, and that loneliness drew me into a defensive, isolating crouch. I spent a lot of time by myself.

Weekends were the worst, for the one thing that kept me tethered to any semblance of stability was my academic routine. Many a weekend night I spent on the phone with a few trusted friends, and then finally my brothers and sisters, crying my eyes out. It wasn't supposed to be this hard! I had already buried my mother and father and the one grandparent I had ever known. I knew what it was like to love and lose. And though I had long accepted the fact that life could be cruel and bitter at times, it seemed ludicrous to have to walk that lonely road severed from my loved ones all because I had made a promise to obey my religious superiors.

Folks often ask me how we are to discern God's will for us. I tell them that we must always discern first what *our* heart's deepest desire is, and having done that, we will discover what *God's* deepest desire is for us as well.

At first I thought my deepest desire was to return to Oakland and go to as many A's games as possible. I thought my heart's deepest desire was to take a bottle of California wine to Baker Beach at dusk and toast the sun as it slipped behind the placid Pacific, casting a light both hieratic and profound on the Golden Gate Bridge. I thought my heart's deepest desire was to "get the hell out of Dodge." Every night I prayed to God to instruct me in his ways, to help me make sense of my suffering. Every morning I prayed—actually, demanded—that God let me know, in a timely manner, what I was supposed to do. And every night and every morning the only words I heard from God in my heart were two: "Trust me." And those two words depressed me to the bottom of my soul.

I began to lose weight. When I went home for a quick visit over Thanksgiving weekend, my family thought I had cancer. I finally began to let my brothers in community know that I was in a desperate struggle to survive. Such is the insidious evil of depression that it makes us believe things that aren't true. I thought I was a complete flop in and out of the classroom. I looked at myself in the mirror and observed a failure—a weak, frightened, pathetic creature—despite every assurance by others to the contrary. I simply did not believe them.

Nonetheless, I held on. I had too much in the game now to fold. I was going to see this hand through. "Trust me" was all God would say to me in those dark days. It was a gamble, but I hadn't much else left to lose.

That December, right near the end of the first semester, I met with a mother of one of my seniors. She had asked to see me because she was concerned about her son's academic performance. The boy was not a particularly disciplined student, and he was struggling to maintain a D in my course. I assumed he wasn't faring much better in his other classes.

The mother was not much older than I was. She was a single mom, working two jobs so that her son could attend Catholic high school. At one point in our conversation, after assuring her that I would continue to work with her son so that he would get a passing grade, I began to tell her the potential I saw in his writing. Sure, he was a bit sloppy and inconsistent in his prose, I said, but he had a bit of the poet in him. I showed her some of his writing and pointed out where I saw real promise. With enough hard work and encouragement, I told her, he could be a promising writer.

And then I thanked her. I told her that poets are almost always born first in the hearts of their mothers and that it is usually the case that writers are nurtured by the encouragement of those who love them. In her son's case, it was she who needed to be thanked for tending to a young mind and heart in their most formative period. I thanked her for being a great mom.

Suddenly, she began to cry. I knew immediately that they were tears of both joy and sadness.

I realized that she was hearing—maybe for the first time in a long, long time—that she was not a failure, that she really was doing an amazing job raising her son all on her own. I saw sadness because maybe she had come perilously close to surrendering to the darkness of despair.

"Fr. Pat," she said, "there's something you need to know, something none of John's classmates know. Tomorrow," she continued, "John will be celebrating his first year of sobriety. He is a recovering heroin addict."

She proceeded to tell me of her son's middle school years, when he had first experimented with marijuana and alcohol, and how in the eighth grade he had gotten hooked on heroin. She told me of his slow progress and how grateful he was to be at Notre Dame because it placed a healthy distance between him and those whom he associated with during his drinking and drugging days. She told me that he was so looking forward to the next day, when he would celebrate his "first birthday" off drugs.

By the end of our conversation we both were in tears, and afterward it began to dawn on me that maybe God had indeed answered my prayers. Perhaps I now knew why I had been asked to move to Chicago. Perhaps it was my heart's deepest desire to stay. In one brief encounter with the mother of one of my students, both of our sufferings had been laid bare, and for both of us, the suffering had become redemptive.

Thomas Merton often talked about the idea of redemptive suffering. For Christians, suffering of any sort becomes redemptive when we willingly hand it over to God, trusting in the healing power of the redeeming cross of his Son, Jesus Christ.

John's mother and I had walked alone for a long time up our separate Calvary hills, until—at that one graced time—we began to walk together.

Those first months at Notre Dame were for me three long days in the tomb. I was asked by my superiors to come to Chicago so that—unbeknownst to them or to me—I might come to trust God more completely. I had to leave home and loved ones in order to see my familial and tribal predisposition for melancholy as a gift of sorts and not a burden.

At the end of Mark's Gospel, when the three women arrive at the tomb of Jesus only to find that the huge stone covering the entrance has been rolled away, they see a young man in a white robe sitting on the right side of the tomb. "Do not be amazed!" the young man urges them. "You seek Jesus of Nazareth, the crucified. He has been raised; he is not here."

Five years ago, I was swallowed by a deep darkness, and for a while I lay helpless in a tomb. And then one day, a young man, one who had spent a year putting on new garments of sobriety, garments that would heal the syringe marks on his body and make him new again, rolled the stone away for me. His name was John, and he was the angel who came to tell me that there was reason to trust, to hope, to hold on.

Shadow of the Father

Paul Mariani

from *America*

How shall I approach you, Joseph, you, the shadow
of the Father? The stories vary. But who
were you, really? Were you young? Old?

A widower, with children of your own, as the *Proto-
evangelium* says? I have been to bloody Bethlehem
and seen the orphaned children there.

A small town, where Palestinian gunmen roamed the Church
of the Nativity, while Israeli snipers watched
from the adjoining rooftops. It is a scene not all that

different from Herod's horsemen hunting down a baby,
though you, dreamer that you were, had already heeded
the midnight warning and fled with Mary and the baby,

and though they failed him, you found him, Joseph,
and raised him, teaching him your trade, two day laborers
who must often have queued up, looking for work.

How difficult it must have been, standing in, as every father
    must sometimes feel. But where else did your Son find
      his courage and sense of outrage against injustice,

how did he become the man he was, if not for you? "Didn't
    you know
    I had to be about my father's business?" Thus the boy,
      at twelve,
      there in Jerusalem. Words which must have wounded

though they put the matter in its proper light. After that,
    you drop
    from history. Saint of happy deaths, was yours a happy
      death?
      Tradition says it was, logic seems to say it was,

with that good woman and that sweet son there by your
    side. For the past
    two months my wife and her sister have been caring for
      their
      father, who is dying of cancer. There is the hospital
      bed,

the potty, the rows of medicine to ease the growing pain.
    From time
    to time he starts up from his recliner to count his
      daughters
      and his aged Irish bride, thinking of a future he no
      longer

has. When she was little, my wife once told me, she prayed
daily
in the church of St. Benedict to St. Joseph that she might
have a daily missal. One day, a man in coveralls

came up to her and without a word gave her one with your
name
on it. Oh, she said, her parents would never allow it.
Put a penny in the poor box, then, he said, and

turned and disappeared forever. Who was he? I asked.
You know as well as I do who he was, is all she'd say.
Joseph, be with her now, and with her father, as he
faces

the great mystery, as we all must at the end, alone. You seem
like so many other fathers, who have watched over
their families, not knowing what the right words were,

but willing to be there for them, up to the very end. Be with
them now,
as you have been for countless others. Give them
strength.
And come, if need be, in a dream, as the angel came
to you,

and came to the other Joseph in Egypt so many years before.
Be there
as once you were in Queens and Bethlehem and
Nazareth.
You, good man, dreamer, the shadow of the Father.

Harry Potter, Catholic Boy

John O'Callaghan

from *Portland Magazine*

Scholastic Books, the American publisher of the Harry Potter novels, changed the title of the first book from its British title, *Harry Potter and the Philosopher's Stone,* to *Harry Potter and the Sorcerer's Stone*—American readers apparently cannot be expected to buy a book with *philosopher* in the title. But this change misled many to think that the novels were fundamentally about sorcery, witches, and witchcraft. They're not. They are about philosophy, literally "the love of wisdom," the desire to understand better the highest causes of things, and they are about faith seeking understanding, *fides quaerens intellectum,* in the lovely Latin phrase. These two themes are intertwined and have an ancient heritage in Western culture, from Plato and Aristotle through Augustine and Aquinas to J. K. Rowling, who gives narrative expression to them in a lively morality tale, pitting unfettered power and evil against the power of goodness and love, a culture of life versus a culture of death in search of the philosopher's treasure: wisdom.

Consider the rich religious symbols used throughout the novels. We have the character of Lucius Malfoy—that is, Lucifer, surnamed "bad faith." We have his son, Draco, whose name is Latin for "snake." We have Slytherin House, again the snake. By contrast we have Gryffindor House, *griffin d'or* being French for "golden griffin"—a medieval symbol of Christ. We have, in the third novel, *The Prisoner of Azkaban,* Lupin, the wolf, symbol of poverty and of St. Francis (the association with St. Francis is apt when we think of Professor Lupin's ill health and the rags he wears for clothes), and Sirius Black, the dog, which represents "watchfulness and fidelity," often used in religious art as a symbol of St. Dominic and associated with the Dominicans (who are known as the Blackfriars because of the black capes they wear over their white religious habits). And the villain of the third book is Peter Pettigrew, the rat, symbol of destruction and evil.

Most striking of images in the books is the deer or stag, which represents piety, religious aspiration, solitude, and purity of life. Unbeknownst to Harry, it is his father in the form of a stag who appears when he utters the *Expecto patronum* spell in the third book. Recall that Harry is passing out, about to be overcome by the kiss of a Dementor (themselves unsubtle tributes to J. R. R. Tolkien's Ringwraiths). In Latin, *patronus* means "defender" or "advocate" and is etymologically linked with the Latin for "father." *Expecto* means "I await," a waiting that may be tinged with hope, as in the Nicene Creed's *expecto resurrectionem.* So the spell *Expecto patronum* means "I await a defender, an advocate." It turns out that the answer to Harry's prayer is the father whom he hopes for. The son is saved by his prayer and then sees himself standing next to the stag on the bank across the lake. Later the wise Dumbledore explains, "Your father is alive in you, Harry, and shows himself most plainly when you have need of him . . . "

Perhaps the most dramatic and striking symbol in *The Philosopher's Stone,* however, is the unicorn slaughtered by Voldemort. The unicorn in medieval art was a symbol of purity; legend had it that only a virgin could capture a unicorn. The unicorn would run to the virgin, lay its head in her lap, and fall asleep. For obvious reasons it was also personified as a symbol of the Virgin Mary and Jesus. When Hagrid and the children tell Ronan the centaur that a unicorn has been injured in the forest, Ronan responds by saying, "Always the innocent are the first victims. . . . So it has been for ages past, so it is now." Seen in a religious light and with the association with Mary and Jesus, these words remind the reader of the slaughter of the Holy Innocents at the hands of Herod.

Voldemort's name means "one who wills death." But he does not will death for himself; he wants the eternal life that he believes the Philosopher's Stone will grant him. No, he wills the death of others as the means to this eternal life. That is why he slaughtered the unicorn and tried to slaughter Harry. In the climactic scene he explains to Harry that ideas of good and evil are youthful and "ridiculous." He says, "There is no good and evil, there is only power, and those too weak to seek it." For the attentive reader, this is a direct reference to Nietzsche, who argued that this will to power is at the heart of philosophy and is the secret desire of the modern quest for absolute autonomy. And yet the authentic love of his mother protects Harry and conquers this quest for unfettered power. Good, which is associated with love, triumphs over evil.

Finally, the mythic symbol of Dumbledore is the phoenix, another medieval symbol of Christ because of its ability to rise from the ashes on the third day after it has been consumed in a holocaust. It is the phoenix that comes to Harry in the Chamber of Secrets when he recalls Dumbledore's promise to remain at Hogwarts as long as someone there thinks of him. The phoenix gives Harry the gift of the sword of Godric Gryffindor, with which he will slay the Basilisk. The name Godric is a pre–Norman Conquest English name that means "the power of God." So we have in the scene the association of two symbols of Christ, the phoenix and the griffin. And the gift the phoenix gives Harry is the power of God, the power of Christ, to slay the Basilisk, a symbol of Satan.

In short: Hogwarts is not a school of sorcery and the occult mastery of nature. It is a school of virtue, a community of inquiry in pursuit of wisdom, an academy of philosophy.

Deliver Us from Evil

Ferdinand Oertel

from *St. Anthony Messenger*

I was six years old when Hitler came into power. At that time, in January 1933, there was one Nazi Party member among the two thousand people in our village, and Hitler seemed far away.

I grew up in Flittard, a village so named because it was founded on the "flowing banks" of the Rhine, in a rural area in western Germany. On clear days we could see the high spires of Cologne's Gothic cathedral, ten miles to the south. On days with strong winds from the east, we were inundated with stinking yellow fumes from the Bayer aspirin factory to the north.

Our village was poor and Catholic. In the center of Flittard was our church, and in the church was a great mosaic showing God the Pantocrator, the creator of all, with large, penetrating eyes. We knew God was omniscient and omnipotent, and that we lived on earth to do his will and by that gain eternal joys in heaven. I was not the only village child with dreams haunted by God's all-seeing eyes.

Life in our village followed the rules and rhythms of the church, with common daily prayers in families, abstinence from meat on Fridays, and fasting from Ash Wednesday through Good Friday. Traditional processions paraded around the village on the Feast of the Ascension and Corpus Christi.

But the people in my village were not saints. There was swindling in selling land and goods, violence among men when they were drunk, even adultery. Yet everyone knew about nearly every case; in fact, almost everyone was related and there were no secrets among us. Those who did wrong knew it was wrong.

I believe that our Catholic traditions and rhythm of life prevented people in our village from becoming caught up in the Nazi movement. And it was also because of a young chaplain appointed to our village who became an example of fearlessly facing evil.

Hitler came into our village by radio on January 30, 1933. At the beginning of that year, the president of the Weimar Republic, Paul von Hindenburg, a widely admired, unpolitical field marshal of World War I, had nominated Adolf Hitler to become the new chancellor of Germany.

At that time, Germany was in political and economic crisis. Defeated in World War I, the country was burdened by the victorious Allies with huge reparations and was still recovering from the bank crash in 1929. Millions of people were unemployed. The transition from monarchy to democratic government had failed due to a great number of divided and selfish political parties. In this situation, Adolf Hitler and his National Socialist Party played on the anxieties of the masses.

Immediately after Hitler's nomination, he wanted to make a radio address to the nation. My uncle living next door was our only relative to own a radio. He came over and placed it on a cupboard in the living room of my grandparents' house, where all the family members gathered for the transmission from Berlin. On this occasion, I, for the first time, heard the voice of Adolf Hitler, but I could hardly understand a word because of his strange dialect and his hysterical outbursts.

In his hypnotizing voice, Hitler told the German people that he would restore their national honor by abolishing the disgrace of the Treaty of Versailles (1919). Many patriotic Germans believed the Allies had unjustly exploited Germany with this peace treaty, which had ended World War I.

Hitler promised employment for everyone and to expel all "criminal creatures" of non-Aryan races who, according to him, spoiled the superior German *Volksgemeinschaft* (community of people).

I recall three reactions to this speech. My father, who had served with the army in World War I at the western front, murmured, "Finally he will restore the reputation of our soldiers." My uncle, who was one of the millions of unemployed, shouted joyfully, "We'll all get jobs!" My grandfather, who had experienced the monarchy and several short-lived, unstable democratic governments, repeated in a warning voice the slogan of the Socialist in the last free election, "Hitler means war again . . ."

Life in our village went on in familiar patterns. I joined the Catholic Youth Organization and eagerly took part in its activities, ranging from adoration hours in the church to camp vacation in the nearby forests.

We barely noticed that many adults in our village secretly were becoming members of the Nazi Party. They seemed ashamed of this and seldom wore the round badge with the swastika in public, but they were compelled by the Nazi state authorities to join the party to keep their jobs. They regarded—rightly or wrongly—their dual membership in the church and the Nazi Party as a necessary concession in order to make a living.

Then, just as Adolf Hitler and the Nazi Party were receiving great international attention for their organization of the 1936 Olympic Games in Berlin, our local Nazi leader tried to co-opt the Catholic youth in our village.

I recall events that showed opposition was possible—in one way or another. In all cases, Chaplain Hugo Poth, our new adviser, played a decisive role. He had been appointed to our parish at the age of thirty, and we young people immediately became his close friends. He understood our way of thinking and speaking.

In catechism lessons, he turned our picture of God from a strong God the Father with penetrating eyes to the mild face of his Son, Jesus our redeemer. He assured us that God would help us find the right way in all times of temptation (hinting at the Nazi ideology without calling it by name).

The local Nazi Party leader tried to draw all schoolboys ages eight, nine, or ten years old away from the Catholic Youth Organization and into the Hitler Youth by organizing a Sunday camp near the Rhine River. This was a tempting offer.

Chaplain Hugo, however, intervened subtly yet effectively. He started by asking the leader, who always wore the Hitler uniform and was a well-known soccer player, whether we would have an opportunity at the camp to attend Mass on Sunday morning. Fulfilling this obligation was guaranteed by the Hitler government in the 1933 concordat with the Holy See. "You wouldn't want to disturb this relationship, would you?" Chaplain Hugo asked.

The leader hesitated and then said to the chaplain: "All right, I could arrange the camp on Saturdays instead of Sundays. Or what would you advise me to do for the boys? I have an order to recruit them for the Hitler Youth."

Chaplain Hugo, of course, had an idea: he alluded to the leader being an excellent soccer player and suggested he organize a soccer team—knowing that most of the Catholic boys did not like soccer and that the games were played on Saturdays.

Taking this advice, the leader established a Hitler soccer team in our village with a dozen boys who were not part of Catholic Youth, and we could remain active in our organization.

Soon rivalries and fights developed, as often happens among boys, but we found a way to maintain our identity without violence. On one Saturday, the Hitler Youth formation was marching to the soccer field when we met them while coming from a retreat. Seeing us, the Hitler boys started to sing defiantly one of the propaganda songs of the Hitler Youth: "We follow the flag with the swastika." Immediately our chaplain started singing the Catholic Youth song: "We carry the banner of Christ." We all joined in loudly.

This led to what could be called a *Sängerkrieg,* a "singers' war"—a spirited but nonviolent competition among singers.

By 1934, members of the Catholic Youth Organization could not wear their uniforms in public. A year later, the Nazis forced all young people into the Nazi youth groups.

By 1938, the Nazi regime had reached the top of its power. It enlarged the German territory by occupying Austria and parts of Czechoslovakia without resistance from the Allies. Following their racial theory, the Nazis not only put political enemies, homosexuals, and Jews in concentration camps but also started euthanizing mentally and physically handicapped people as "not worth living."

Pope Pius XI protested against these criminal acts of the Nazis in his encyclical *With Burning Anxiety.* Several German bishops condemned the actions against the Jews and handicapped. But the Nazis tried to suppress any publication of these Catholic protests. There were, however, many private Catholic printers who secretly made copies of the pope's encyclical and the bishops' sermons, and we Catholic Youth distributed them at night.

After the Nazis invaded Poland in September 1939, they intensified their raids on the Jews. Until then, we knew of the imprisonment of the Jews only by hearsay because there was just one Jew living in our village. She was married to a Catholic clerk who had retired; her only grandson was a friend of mine.

At the end of 1941, after the "blitz" victories in Poland and in France, Nazi leaders decided to exterminate all Jews with their inhuman "Final Solution." One day a rumor spread through our village that the Jewish woman had been arrested the night before and taken to a concentration camp.

Chaplain Hugo saw the local authority of the Nazi department in Cologne, telling him that the old woman was married to a "clean Aryan" German and was of no harm to society. He was assured this would be taken into account.

At the war's end she came back to our village. We found out she had been sent not to an extermination camp but to a working camp. Although she suffered much from hunger, illness, and maltreatment, she had survived the Holocaust and was freed by American troops.

In 1942, after America had joined the Allies, bombing of German arms industries and cities intensified. Everyone in Flittard, and elsewhere in Germany, just wanted to survive the war. We had to spend many hours in a basement shelter in our house. One night a bombing attack intended for the Bayer factory hit apartment houses nearby, killing twelve civilians.

At the same time, almost every day one of the feared letters with a black border was delivered to a family in the village, announcing the death of a soldier son or father. The German army was facing superior Allied troops in Russia, in North Africa, and along the European Atlantic coast. Due to the growing shortage of soldiers, the Nazis started to draft students. Thus, in autumn 1943, when I was not yet sixteen, I had to serve first with an antiaircraft unit near my hometown and then with a military unit in occupied Poland. Luckily, our unit avoided the Russians and managed to be taken prisoner by the British near the Danish border in May 1945. Since I was not yet eighteen, the British released me after only a few months.

It was of great help to me during my two years of military service to receive letters and pamphlets from former Catholic Youth leaders who were living underground and secretly spreading messages of Christian resistance and hope. (One of them was the students' group The White Rose at Munich University, whose members were betrayed before the end of the war and executed by the Nazis.)

Meanwhile, I had scarcely heard from my village during this time. After my return, I was told that in the last days of the war, when the Allied forces were crossing the Rhine River, the Nazis forced all the old men in our village to join special groups to fight tanks. These units were equipped with a new "wonder weapon," a rocket that had to be launched from a man's shoulder, making it difficult and dangerous to handle. My father, who had command of one of these units, succeeded in delaying the operation until his men could surrender to the Allies.

But it was Chaplain Hugo who had saved our village from being destroyed. Carrying a large white sheet as a sign of surrender, he approached the advancing tanks, welcoming the soldiers as the ones who would liberate us from our twelve-year nightmare. He also had asked the remaining people in the village—mostly mothers with children—to put white sheets out on their houses as well. So the American soldiers entered our village without a gunshot.

After my release from the British prison camp in the north, I walked most of the five hundred miles back to Flittard. On the last part of the way I was lucky to get a ride on a pickup from a farmer. After passing the totally destroyed Bayer factory and the city of Leverkusen, I suddenly discovered in the far distance the spire of my village's old church.

The church spire was a symbol to me. Our faith had helped my Catholic family survive the Nazis and their terrorism. As Psalm 125 reads,

The scepter of the wicked will not prevail
   in the land given to the just,
Lest the just themselves
   turn their hands to evil."

Love Is Patient

Robert T. Reilly

from *U.S. Catholic*

When I brought her the valentine, she smiled, but I knew the card was more for me than her. She didn't really know what it said. I read the message aloud, and she smiled again. I had to be satisfied with that.

My wife is one of America's four million Alzheimer's victims. She has had the disease for more than nine years, and until a few months ago, I was her inept caregiver. But you should know her first as a person, not merely a statistic.

We became engaged in 1943, while I was on leave, and Jean then waited almost two years for me to return from the Second World War. She wrote me every day, even when I was missing in action and she had no idea if I was alive or dead. My first message to her was a cable from the liberty ship carrying me home after I was wounded and a prisoner of war.

When we docked in Boston, I phoned her at the Omaha airport, where she was working as one of United Airlines' first female passenger agents. They were experiencing a power failure and ticketing passengers by candlelight. Her colleagues melted away so that I could use this romantic situation to set a wedding date—just two weeks away. Somehow she made it work.

Still in uniform, I needed no tux, and Jean fashioned little organdy hats to accent her bridesmaids' former prom dresses. Her wedding gown was borrowed, and her airline friends pooled their sugar ration coupons so the United chef could create a proper wedding cake for the reception at her folks' house.

That was fifty-seven years ago, years that involved several moves, a few different jobs, and ten children. We tested our wedded bliss in a series of military posts—Texas, Arkansas, Washington—always worrying if we'd be able to locate affordable housing. After I returned to civilian life, we spent four years in a Massachusetts housing project while I worked on a graduate degree and earned twenty-five dollars a week as an ad agency copywriter.

Our first child, Kathleen, was born deaf, a result of rubella. Because we had no car, Jean volunteered as a Red Cross driver so that she could have access to one, allowing her to take our daughter to a special school in Boston.

In 1950, we returned to Omaha and raised our children there. Besides Kathleen being deaf, three of our youngsters had severe asthma, and another had an eye tumor removed at the Mayo Clinic. Like many other postwar couples, Jean and I lived from paycheck to paycheck. Through these challenging years, Jean bore the major domestic responsibilities, always without complaint. People remarked on her serenity, her ability to calmly address each new problem. I learned to admire her instinctive wisdom.

One day a trio of neighborhood boys was teasing Kathleen about her handicap. I was ready to knock their heads together, but Jean intervened, betting them that Kathleen could outrun them. They laughed at this challenge, but Kathleen, always a speedster, won the race.

Jean made peace like that all the time, effortlessly. If I complained about some contemporaries who apparently had it easier than we did, she'd sagely comment, "They're not dead yet."

I could add more evidence and anecdotes, but you get the idea. Jean was always counseling our children about their decisions, consoling and supporting them even when they opted erroneously. She also knew me better than I knew myself.

All of these qualities made it seem doubly unjust when she developed Alzheimer's.

I knew a little about the disease. My sister-in-law's husband had it and would often wander. She'd phone me and I'd jump in the car and track him to one of his haunts. One of my closest friends in the army became a Lutheran minister, a kind and sensitive church leader. When he got the disease, however, his wife had to put him in a home because he became belligerent, completely out of character. The wife of another friend suffered for many years before dying. When I wrote him about my wife's Alzheimer's, soliciting advice, all he wrote back was "God help you."

It is true, however, that "once you've met one Alzheimer's patient, you've met one Alzheimer's patient," so Jean's condition had its own unique character. And it came on very slowly.

I would tell her something and she would later insist I hadn't mentioned the matter. I'd think that perhaps I did neglect to convey that information. I should have seen this as an early sign of dementia, but I put it down to aging on both our parts. When she couldn't find her way home one evening, it scared her—and me—so she stopped driving. Shortly thereafter she became disoriented in an airport, heading for the planes instead of back to where I was sitting, awaiting her return from the restroom. I knew then we had to get the professionals involved.

After several exams the doctor confirmed the Alzheimer's diagnosis. I never left her alone after that.

I suppose it would be easy to recite some of the more bizarre results of the disease, but they don't mirror the whole story. Let's just say that Alzheimer's affects every aspect of your relationship. Your lives merge more than ever. Your biographies become more unified. In Scripture we read that to save your life you must lose your life. In a twisted sense, this happens to both the patient and the caregiver. Sometimes I felt as if I was living my life in fifteen-minute spurts.

Of course, you have to be careful. Professionals warn that you can do no good if you get down yourself. "I've lost more caregivers than Alzheimer's victims," one physician cautioned me. I can see how this happens. Although you love the person you're helping, you also realize that things will only get worse. It took me several years, a quadruple bypass, and a few strokes to come to terms with this.

Your faith sustains you, of course, but you have to work at that harder, too. I suppose a saint could offer it all up. And that's why there are so few saints.

How do you describe a day-to-day scenario? Some years ago I had lunch with the late actor Pat O'Brien, who gave me a memorable line. A priest friend of his had described hearing the confessions of nuns as "being stoned to death with popcorn." Sometimes the caregiver's role is like that. No major tantrums or hallucinations but, rather, a series of small difficulties.

Like things being moved to unfamiliar locales. The sugar bowl travels to the freezer, bananas join the silverware, dirty clothes fraternize with the clean. The Alzheimer's patient might want to help with the cooking and mix peanut butter with the eggs and then burn that concoction. Or fill the steam iron with liquid starch. Or fold everything in sight, making fifty neat squares out of a toilet paper roll.

It amazed me how many different ways there were not to take three pills. Take one, leave two. Take two, leave one.

Leave all three. Take three and spit them into a glass. It takes practice to get them swallowed.

I found I had to monitor her television viewing because she had a tough time distinguishing between screen images and reality. She might call me to help a man who had fallen in a TV drama. Or walk over, crying, and stroke the set when someone died. I resorted to programming comedies.

She began humming or singing, a fairly common practice for those with dementia. I've read that the last thing a person loses is music. Friends might say, "Well, it's better than screaming or crying." That argument is difficult to appreciate when you are exposed to something like tinnitus sans melody. Even Pavarotti might become less enjoyable after a few steady hours.

It's hard to define a day. There is some routine, some change, gradual loss, no real recovery. The day is dictated by the moods and needs of the person in your care. You realize you must answer all phone calls yourself, check the doors at night, make all the decisions. You find it hard to make the king-size bed alone. You miss the sharing of ideas and responsibilities. You may also resent never being able to relax, never allowing yourself to feel unwell, never being able to confidently interpret communication. And you're never certain that what you're doing is right.

We have six children still in town, and they have been a great help. But they have lives of their own, and I hesitate to impose too much. Groups like the Alzheimer's Association offer all sorts of help. But I suppose it is a curse of my generation that we try to solve things ourselves.

I acknowledge my lack of professional skills, but I did bring things to the table: I loved the patient; I had a history with her; I understood her needs, knew her likes and dislikes; I provided familiarity and security and a certain level of comfort. I knew the house and environment. I was a link to a past already damaged.

I read an article in *Harper's* by a woman who had responsibility for her mother, whose Alzheimer's was accelerating. The writer used the metaphor of someone on a failed Arctic exploration, concluding by saying she felt alone in her tent, the wind howling outside, and, having eaten the last of her sled dogs, tried to sleep, uncertain if morning would come. It was the grimmest piece I'd ever read on caregiving. I noted that she had no sort of faith to sustain her.

I believe you need one of three things to succeed as a caregiver: love, faith, or duty. It works best if you have all three.

There are many variations of love, but I'm not talking about the kind that flares up and burns brightly for a time. I mean the kind you can bank like a good fire against the certain cold and dark.

And duty. I was brought up respecting duty, which means you continue to do something even when the reasons have dissipated. Call it commitment.

And you can't make it without faith. You have to get your strength from somewhere, and you have to be convinced that God knows what's going on. You must believe that someday and somewhere everything will be put right and your bruised relationship will be whole again. You have to trust that everything happens for a reason, even though you can't fathom it. I believe that God scrutinized me and concluded I wasn't a bad guy, merely a little driven, somewhat impatient. So he's teaching me that virtue.

I pray, of course, but not for cures or miracles. I pray for my wife's continued health and serenity and for my own understanding. I pray that our children will also come to terms with the situation and not fret about this cross being visited on a wonderful mother or this disease tearing apart a couple still very much in love. I want them to know that God doesn't wish suffering on anyone.

David Karp, a sociologist and the author of *The Burden of Sympathy* (Oxford University Press), gives this advice: "The people who are most successful in this caregiving situation are those who have truly internalized the mantra of the caregiving group I've been observing, something they call the Four Cs—'I didn't cause it; I can't cure it; I can't control it; I can only cope with it.'"

I'd add that you can also pray about it. And I try to remember how life must be for the person with Alzheimer's. It's facile to say they really don't know what's going on, but many of them do.

A friend was visiting us, and my wife, seated next to me, was babbling nonsense phrases, making no sense. The friend then mentioned she had two children, and my wife asked, out of the blue, "How old are they?"

After constant urgings by my doctor, friends, and family and a few months' trial with limited day care, I finally agreed to some sort of permanent professional care. I'm sure I should have surrendered to this earlier, not for my sake but for hers. She now lives all on one floor, not on six levels like in our house. There are grab bars in strategic places and no rugs to trip on, and all potentially dangerous things are locked away. Professional caregivers are on duty around the clock, and both a nurse and a therapist come in daily. Jean adjusted quickly. I'm still working it out. Despite the warmth of the caregivers, I still feel a bit like a guest.

Most days, Jean just sits there beside me, rests her head on my shoulder, and dozes. Sometimes there is arrested communication. I show her photos, sing to her, talk softly. On Sundays

I bring her communion, but, more and more, she seems unaware of what she is doing. I feel caught between sacrament and sacrilege.

One day the nurse said, "I tear up every time I see how excited she is to see you."

"Listen," I told her, "for sixty years that's the way I felt when she walked into a room." The nurse cried at that.

So I stumble along, learning, at age eighty, to fashion a new life. Jean is doing the same. I suppose someday the other residents will be realer than any past we shared. When that time comes, I hope I'm ready.

To pull myself out of a lonely funk, I tell myself how hard it was to be the sole caregiver, but I honestly can't remember those burdens. It's like the Scripture passage where the woman forgets the pain of childbirth in the joy that a child is born.

I build my days around visits to her, not as corporal works of mercy but as one of the joys of marriage. I love who she was, but I also love who she is.

And I have evidence that God isn't absent. Take the subject of money, for example. Alzheimer's care is expensive, and normally I couldn't afford it. However, some thirty-five years ago my wife talked me into buying a cabin in Colorado, reminding me that the place was worth far more than the asking price. The family enjoyed that cabin for twenty summers, and Jean loved it most of all. We sold the place for far more than we'd paid, and those dollars are now paying for her care. Some might call it coincidence or serendipity, but I prefer to believe that God had his own long-term care plan.

The caregiver years were hard. But I'm glad I had the chance to do something for my wife, who had done so much for me. Those years also revealed me in a new favorable light to my children. And I learned a great deal.

Even on the most difficult days, there were rewards. One day I had taken Jean and a sister-in-law to a restaurant. I left them for a minute to chat with friends at another table. While I was absent, my wife said to my sister-in-law, pointing at me, "That's the man who takes care of me."

That night, as a test, I asked Jean, "Who am I?" She didn't seem to understand my question. So I asked again, "What's my name?" She thought for a few seconds and replied, "You're my darling."

When I was weighing the option of full-time care, the woman in charge of the home told me, "You won't feel good about the decision when you make it. And you won't feel good about it a year later." She's partially right. Intellectually, I know I acted responsibly; emotionally, I'm working on it. I told my pastor last February that this would be the best Lent I ever made because I'd given up the thing that meant most to me in the world.

I have a certain conviction that we will be together again and as we used to be. I have had dreams about that final reunion. I've seen it in my mind a hundred times. We're both dressed in white, and we're dancing in front of patio doors that are open to a sea.

Many writers have dubbed Alzheimer's "the long good-bye." But I think there is no good-bye, only what I say to Jean at the end of each visit: "I'll see you tomorrow."

I think of the words of Edmond Rostand's Cyrano de Bergerac: "I am never away from you. Even now, I shall not leave you. In another world, I shall be still the one who loves you, loves you beyond measure."

Meanwhile, family, friends, and caring professionals sustain me. On occasion, I am reminded, in nonmiraculous fashion, that my pain is not unnoticed by God.

It was our wedding anniversary. Number fifty-seven. I brought roses to the home and a tape of Beethoven piano concerti. When the professional staff said she sometimes had trouble getting to sleep, I suggested classical music. We often listened to symphonic works together. It worked—my one contribution to the treatment regimen.

Along with the flowers and the tape, I gave her a card, one with a Hebrew phrase that translated, "You will never be out of my heart." I spoke with her about the anniversary and how much these years had meant to me, hoping she would recognize the significance of the date. Her expression said nothing and she didn't reply. Not even a smile of acknowledgment. I returned home a little sad, wishing that God had given her just a fleeting glimpse of what had occurred. No chance.

That night, Mickie, one of the caregivers, phoned me.

"Bob," she said, "she knows it's your anniversary. She was looking at the flowers and the cards, and she said, 'I forgot our anniversary. Is he still here?' I told her you'd be back tomorrow. Then I read her your card and she cried. I cried, too."

I know how she felt. But there is a difference between tears and tears of joy.

Editor's note: Jean McKenzie Reilly died on February 29, 2004. Robert Rielly, her husband of fifty-nine years, died six weeks later, on April 14. In their last weeks together their ten children pushed their beds together so they could hold hands until the end.

The Present Crisis through the Lens of the Laity

Margaret O'Brien Steinfels

from *Commonweal*

Editor's note: Steinfels's talk was delivered to the national meeting of the United States Catholic bishops on June 13, 2002, in Dallas, Texas.

"The gates of hell will not prevail against it." A dramatic and comforting idea to a child growing up in the 1940s and 1950s. And what were the gates of hell?

In that cold war era, they were the forces of persecution. Out there. Confronting us. In Eastern Europe. In Communist China. These were the successors to the Roman emperors, creating modern martyrs.

I grew older. I went to Catholic schools, good Catholic schools, Chicago Catholic schools. In addition to learning many admirable things (like, I learned to love the church), I learned about bad popes. I learned about the sale of indulgences. I learned, from the sisters, about Joan of Arc, tried by a church court and burned alive for heresy and witchcraft. Eventually I learned about full-scale persecutions that we, not they, had conducted. The gates of hell, it turned out, were not only "out there," but also "in here."

And though the church taught, and I believed, that the gates of hell would not prevail, I also learned that the church could do grievous damage to itself, so that in nations long Catholic and among people long Christianized, the gospel no longer was heard and the sacraments were no longer received.

I grew still older, and I learned that the gates of hell were not necessarily the despair-inducing gateway of Dante's *Inferno* ("Abandon all hope, ye who enter here") or the fire-encircled, monster-guarded gates of Milton's imagination. The gates of hell could also be modest, undramatic, everyday passages through which we slip as easily by a furtive act of accommodation, cowardice, silence, or sloth as by some bold act of rebellion. I discovered the gates of hell not only in the bad popes but also in the good yet righteous and narrow-minded ones, not only in corrupt Catholics but in evasive and conformist ones as well. I discovered, as we all eventually do, the gates of hell in my own commissions and omissions.

The current scandal, though overwhelming, is not then a novelty in the history of God's people. Faced with the daunting task of speaking to you at a time like this, I turned to a book I admire, written in the late forties by the French theologian Henri de Lubac. *The Splendor of the Church* is a book that foreshadowed much of Vatican II, and by its unflinching honesty made clear why a Vatican II was so necessary.

We are all human, de Lubac begins one passage—actually he wrote, "We are all men," but I made this one slight adjustment—"and there is none of us but is aware of his own wretchedness and incapacity; for after all we keep on having our noses rubbed in our own limitations. We have all, at some time or other, caught ourselves red-handed . . . trying to serve a holy cause by dubious means. . . . So that there are scanty grounds for making exceptional cases of ourselves; and none at all for the withdrawal implied in a grimly-judging eye. If we behave in that way, we fall into an illusion like that of the misanthrope, who takes a dislike to humankind, for all the world as if he himself were not a part of it."

It is when we cease to hold ourselves apart with "a grimly judging eye," de Lubac writes, that "the staring contrast between the human wretchedness of those who make up the Church, and the greatness of her divine mission, will no longer be a scandal to us; for we shall first have become painfully aware of [that wretchedness] in ourselves. Rather, it will become a stimulus. We shall understand how a certain sort of [self-]criticism which is always directed outwards may be nothing more than a search for an alibi designed to enable us to dodge the examination of our consciences. And a humble acceptance of Catholic solidarity will perhaps be more profitable to us in the matter of shaking us out of some of our illusions."

You can understand why I found that passage so appropriate. We come here aware of our wretchedness, having had our noses rubbed in our limitations, knowing that we have served a holy cause by dubious means, hoping that the very contrast between our wretchedness and the church's mission may guard us against forms of (self-)criticism that are only a search for alibis.

But it is de Lubac's presiding note of "humble acceptance of Catholic solidarity" that captured me above all. That solidarity has been brought home day after day to millions of Catholics as—with dread—we pick up the newspaper. In the best of times, the news is excruciatingly full of victims—but these are the church's victims, our victims, and the church's victimizers, our victimizers. Solidarity has seldom been so painful, so difficult to sustain, so humbling, or, in the end, so important. Certainly responsibility for the present crisis in the Catholic Church in the United States rests more squarely on some shoulders than others—and responsibility for responding to it does as well. But, with de Lubac's help, I come fighting the temptation to separate myself, to address "you others" rather than us, to employ the grimly judging eye so congenial to editors.

That is not the only temptation we must fight.

We are tempted, for example, to imagine that this crisis is going to be swiftly and conclusively resolved by decisive action at this meeting. Decisive action is, of course, essential. It means that the church will not be in worse shape when you leave than when you arrived. But we know that even the best policy on paper must be implemented. We know that there remains a backlog of abuse cases to be addressed. We know that wounds have been opened, anger provoked, suspicions planted, and questions raised that cannot be dealt with here and now—but must be dealt with over time, conscientiously and purposefully.

What if we left here having really absorbed the idea that the Catholic Church in the United States will never be the same? We would know then that what is done here today and tomorrow can only be a down payment on what you—and what all of us—must do over years to come.

We are also tempted to imagine that this scandal has not touched our faith. Do you find grim comfort in polls showing that between 75 and 80 percent of the Catholic population merely blame you bishops rather than question their faith? But what about the one or two in ten who does question it? But would that even be all! We know that faith can be challenged by tragedy and personal crisis, weakened by mobility, and rendered complicated by intermarriage. It will be at moments of distress, despair, dissatisfaction, and disagreement—when faith is already under strain—that the legacy of this scandal will be felt, another source of doubt, a ready source of disgust, an easy source of cynicism.

Think for a moment of what a central event Vatican II was in most of our lives—eye opening, mind shaping, formative in multiple ways. Historian John McGreevy has pointed out that especially for the generation of young Catholics already tending toward detachment, this scandal is, in effect, their Vatican II. How crucial, then, the ending of this story.

A third temptation is to blame outside forces rather than examine our own consciences. The media. Anti-Catholicism. Political groups working to discredit the voice of the Catholic Church in public life. Plaintiffs' lawyers. Insurance companies. Blaming others is a natural impulse—an impulse most American church officials have resisted, thankfully. The problem, of course, is that outside forces have played a role in making this scandal what it has become, sometimes for good reasons, sometimes for dubious ones. No honest chronicle could avoid noting that. But no honest appraisal of responsibility would let that become an alibi.

Finally, we are tempted to view this crisis only in institutional terms. What are the consequences for parishes, seminaries, hospitals, soup kitchens, and shelters? For numbers and finances, for vocations and benefactors? We should worry, of course; that is pastorally responsible. But we must recognize that what has happened is a terrible blow to the church's witness in the culture, a blow to its credibility in proclaiming the Good News, a blow to its ability in the public square to assist the poor, to protect the vulnerable, to help the immigrant. Who will listen when Catholics offer their well-developed theological and philosophical vocabulary to civic debates over war and peace, debt relief, the economy, welfare reform, stem-cell research?

Whatever is accomplished at this meeting, then, can only be a beginning.

In thinking about what must yet be done, I keep coming back to two central topics: truth and trust. Obviously they are related. Today laypeople lack trust because they lack truth. And they cannot find the truth because they no longer have trust in their bishops.

The truth is that we don't know the truth, the full truth, about this sex-abuse scandal. Despite the endless reports— sometimes because of the endless reports—we don't know the truth. Yes, we know some truths, and they are horrifying and overwhelming. So overwhelming that we can scarcely keep track of times and places and numbers. But these facts we do know leave many questions unanswered, even unasked. Having read more of these accounts than I wish I had to, I know that the puzzle doesn't fit together. And I believe many of you feel that way, too.

We need to pursue the question *How did we get into this mess?* Given the efforts in many dioceses over the last ten to fifteen years, why are so many people convinced that children are still in danger? Why are people so ready to believe that nothing has been done? People are saddened, even heart-broken, and angered by the violation of children, of course, but also by the violation of the trust they had in their shepherds. Anger seems to increase by the day. And a sense of outrage is almost everywhere accompanied by a sense of utter helplessness.

For beyond the puzzle of what occurred in church decision making, there are the larger questions about deeper causes. There is no end of explanations offered: celibacy, homosexuality, emotional and sexual immaturity, the permissive sixties, the repressive fifties, dissidents, lack of priests, lack of accountability, a clerical club protecting its own, the loss of collegiality. The current crisis has put these topics before us— sometimes glibly, sometimes thoughtfully. Some are controversial, some involve the global church, all are more complicated than most proponents admit, and none can be resolved quickly.

But whatever the causes of the scandal, the fact is that the dam has broken. A reservoir of trust among Catholics has run dry. This scandal has brought home to laypeople how essentially powerless they are to affect its outcome—and virtually anything else to do with the church. When we ask, "What can I do?" what layperson isn't brought up short in realizing, forty years after Vatican II, with its promise of consultation and collaboration, that our only serious leverage is money? That in itself is a scandal.

The dam has broken. Will we ever know the truth? Can trust really be restored? There are many matters that must be discussed: not here, not today—but very soon. Let me be clear: what you must do at this meeting today and tomorrow must not be overwhelmed by these related matters. But clearly the level of mistrust, loss of confidence, and anger flows from more than this scandal.

Bishops are, among other things, guardians of truth. Today you are badly handicapped in this role. How much is due to an active intent to obscure or deceive, how much to responses made without adequate preparation? The fact remains that, in too many instances, some of you have said things that later proved to be contradicted by the facts; you said things that were not true. But not all of you did that. And yet, like the undifferentiated blur of dark deeds, all of you are subject to the same undifferentiated suspicion, the same loss of trust.

Everyone speaks of the loss of trust that this scandal has caused. But what about the loss of trust that preceded it—a loss expressed by both liberals and conservatives, across the spectrum of Catholic views? Why, in other words, had the reservoir of trust run so low?

The causes are many. Secrecy is one. Careerism another. Silent acquiescence in Vatican edicts and understandings that you know to be contrary to your own pastoral experience. Another is a widespread sense of double standards. One standard for what is said publicly and officially, another standard for what is held and said privately. One standard for the baptized, another for the ordained. One standard for priests, another for bishops. One standard for men, another standard for women. One standard for the ordination of heterosexuals, and what now threatens to become another standard for homosexuals. One standard for justice and dialogue outside the church, another for justice and dialogue within.

We all know there are deep differences in the church and in your ranks about the sources and solutions of the crisis. In fact, one side sees as solutions precisely what another sees as sources of the crisis. I know that different groups of Catholics would fill in the specifics in different and often contradictory ways. Still, what all are feeling is a lack of candor, honesty, integrity.

Much has been said and written about the laity's growing distrust of bishops. Let me make note of something else: the hierarchy's distrust of the laity. (I will pass on the issue of your distrust of one another.)

When there is no genuine effort to build accountability and transparency into diocesan and parish governance; when we hear those rote phrases about the church not being a democracy, as if it were a system only of majority vote and not also of checks and balances and of consultation; when we are unilaterally admonished against discussing some topics; when we know that so many bishops and priests cannot or will not say publicly what they really think, especially now, when people long to hear an honest word of explanation; when the Vatican appears to place hopes for priestly vocations in the strict liturgical separation of the ordained and the lay, what conclusion can be drawn except that you don't trust us?

If the laity were trusted, why would so little a real, institutionalized role have developed in parochial and diocesan decision making? Of course, such a role would reflect genuine trust, not blind trust. The wisdom of the Scriptures, Hebrew and Christian, and the wisdom of the church instruct against blind trust. The laity should not have blind trust, nor should bishops—not toward the laity, not toward the clergy, and not toward your fellow bishops.

We can restore trust in the church and in church leadership only if church leadership begins to trust the church—the 99 percent of the church that is the laity. As John Henry Newman observed, "The church would look foolish without them."

We can no longer indulge the slothful habit of postponing the church that we need until the next papacy, until the seminaries are full, until the controversies are resolved, until some faithful remnant rules the church. We need to breathe new life into the project of church renewal that we have neglected for too long. There is much that we must begin to talk about together.

De Lubac, in the passage I quote, urged "a humble acceptance of Catholic solidarity." He concluded, "It will, help us to fall in love once more, from a new standpoint, with those elements in the wisdom and the institutions and the traditions and the demands of our Church which we were coming near to understanding no longer."

The Hour of the Laity

Mary Ann Glendon

from *First Things*

Throughout the twentieth century, leaders of the Catholic Church implored laymen and laywomen with increasing urgency to be more active as Catholics in society and—since Vatican II—to become more involved in the internal affairs of the church. The earlier call found a warm response among Catholic Americans in the 1930s, '40s, and '50s. But as Catholics have gained in affluence and influence, the lay apostolate has suffered, while new opportunities for service in the institutional church have gone begging. No wonder John Paul II, with his history of close collaboration with laymen and laywomen, often refers to the laity as a "sleeping giant." For decades, the giant has seemed lost in the deep slumber of an adolescent. Now that the sleeper is beginning to stir—roused by media coverage of clerical sexual misconduct—it is beginning to look as though the leviathan has the faith IQ of a preadolescent. Can this be the long-awaited "hour of the laity"?

The current resurgence of interest in lay organization suggests that the time is ripe to explore what has happened to American Catholics' understanding of the lay vocation over the years during which they made unprecedented economic and social advances. Are the sixty-three million or so Catholics who make up more than a fifth of the U.S. population evangelizing the culture, as every Christian is called to do, or is the culture evangelizing them?

Since poets and novelists often help us see things afresh, I propose to approach that question through a lens borrowed from an acute literary observer of the modern world. The protagonist of Mario Vargas Llosa's *The Storyteller* is arguably not a person, but a group—a nomadic tribe of rain-forest dwellers. To outsiders, they are known as the Machiguengas, but they call themselves the people-who-walk. We readers never meet the Machiguengas face-to-face; we only hear of them from a narrator who is trying to find out whether the tribe still exists. We learn that from time immemorial, the stories and traditions of the people-who-walk were remembered, enriched, and handed down by *habladors*—storytellers. These stories helped the tribe to maintain its identity—to keep on walking no matter what, through many changes and crises. But as the rain forest gave way to agriculture and industry, the Machiguengas scattered. For a time, their *habladors* traveled from one cluster of families to another and kept them bound together. The storytellers "were the living sap that circulated and made the Machiguengas into a society, a people of interconnected and interdependent beings." But anthropologists think that the storytellers eventually died out, that the Machiguengas were absorbed into cities and villages, and that their stories survive only as entertainment. The narrator suspects otherwise, and the drama of the novel comes from his effort to find out whether it is really true that a mysterious red-haired stranger has become the *hablador* of the Machiguengas so that they will not lose their stories and their sense of who they are.

That problem—of how a dispersed people remembers who it is and what constitutes it as a people—lies at the heart of the challenges confronting the *ecclesia* (which may be translated as "the people-called-together") in America. Catholics are constituted as a people by the story of the world's salvation, and part of that story requires them to be active in the world, spreading the Good News wherever they are. The people-called-together are called to witness, and to keep on witnessing no matter what, in and out of season. How well have American Catholics done at keeping that story alive through the crises, changes, temptations, and opportunities they encountered in the mission territory that is the United States?

From the beginning, Catholic settlers in North America were strangers in a Protestant land. At the time of the founding, several states had established Protestant churches. Congregationalism, for example, was the official religion of Massachusetts until 1833, and in many New England towns the Congregational meetinghouse was the seat of town government as well as the place of Sunday worship. Nevertheless, when Alexis de Tocqueville surveyed the American social landscape in 1831, he predicted that Catholics would flourish there. The growing Catholic presence would prove beneficial for the young nation's experiment in self-government because, he argued, their religion made them "the most democratic class in the United States," since it imposed the same standards on everyone, rich and poor, and it left its followers free to act in the political sphere.

The French visitor, farsighted as he often was, never suspected that a storm was gathering as he wrote those words. He failed to detect the anti-Catholicism that would fuse with nativism and erupt into violence as Catholic immigrants arrived from Europe in ever-increasing numbers. In 1834, an angry mob in Boston (the city he had regarded as America's most civilized) burned an Ursuline convent to the ground while police and firemen stood by and watched. Three years later, arsonists destroyed most of Boston's Irish quarter.

Similar atrocities were repeated across the country. But the expanding economy demanded cheap labor, and the immigrants kept arriving from Ireland, Italy, Germany, French Canada, and Eastern Europe. By the turn of the century, the Roman Catholic Church was the country's largest and fastest-growing religious community, with twelve million adherents.

Struggling for survival in a hostile environment, the immigrant Catholics built their own separate set of primary and high schools, hospitals, and colleges. Picking up on the American penchant for associating, they formed countless fraternal, social, charitable, and professional organizations. Protestants had the Masons and the Eastern Star; Catholics had the Knights of Columbus and the Daughters of Isabella. Through dogged effort and sacrifice, Catholics constructed, in historian Charles Morris's words, "a virtual state-within-a-state so [they] could live almost their entire lives within a thick cocoon of Catholic institutions." From their neighborhood bases in northern cities, the newcomers used democratic political processes to win political power at the state and local levels. But when the Catholic governor of New York ran for president in 1928, virulent anti-Catholicism broke out again. Al Smith's resounding defeat reinforced the Catholic sense of separateness through the 1930s, '40s, and '50s.

Interestingly, the period when Catholic Americans were most separate was the time when they were most active—as Catholics—in the world. In 1931, on the fortieth anniversary of the historic social encyclical *Rerum Novarum,* Pius XI called for Catholic action to counter the transformation of society along communist or fascist lines. "Nowadays," he wrote in *Quadragesimo Anno,* "as more than once in the history of the Church, we are confronted with a world which in large measure has almost fallen back into paganism." He told the lay faithful that they must "lay aside internal quarrels" so that each person could play his role "as far as talents, powers, and station allow" in a peaceful but militant struggle for "the Christian renewal of human society." Laypersons were to be "the first and immediate apostles" in that struggle, he said. The response of Catholics in this country was all that the pope could have wished. They were instrumental in curbing communist influence in the labor movement, and they made the Democratic Party in the urban North into the party of the neighborhood, the family, and the workingman.

The Spanish philosopher George Santayana, who taught at Harvard in the early twentieth century, was intrigued by the contrast between what he perceived as a buoyant, optimistic American culture and the ancient Catholic faith, with its "vast disillusion about this world and minute illusions about the next." He wrote in 1934 that Catholics in the United States had no serious conflicts with their Protestant neighbors because "their respective religions pass among them for family matters, private and sacred, with no political implications." If Santayana had spent less time in Cambridge and more in Boston, he would have realized that the Catholicism of urban immigrant communities was not at all "private"; it was merely enclosed in the neighborhoods. Those were the decades when lay Catholics were intensely involved, as Catholics, in the parish, the workplace, and the precinct. It was also a time when the people-called-together was blessed with an abundance of storytellers. In parochial schools, at Mass and devotions, and around their kitchen tables, Catholics were constantly reminded of who they were, where they came from, and what their mission was in the world.

But as St. Paul told the Corinthians, "The world as we know it is always passing away." As Catholics climbed up the economic and social ladders, they left the old neighborhoods for the suburbs. Parents began sending their children to public schools and to non-Catholic colleges. Vocations to religious life declined. Geographic and social mobility scattered Catholic communities of memory and mutual aid as relentlessly as agriculture and industry pushed back the rain forest of the Machiguengas. By the 1960s, the Catholic nation-within-a-nation had dissolved, and the diaspora had begun.

The people-called-together thus embarked on what Morris well describes as "the dangerous project of severing the connection between the Catholic religion and the separatist . . . culture that had always been the source of its dynamism, its appeal, and its power." The transition was symbolized by the election to the presidency of a highly assimilated Catholic, John F. Kennedy, who matched the nativists in the vigor of his denunciation of public aid to parochial schools. The 1960 election taught ambitious descendants of immigrants that all doors could be open to them so long as they were not too Catholic.

Two years later came the opening of the Second Vatican Council, the church's historic effort to meet the challenges of bringing the gospel to the structures of the modern, increasingly secularized world. The council fathers, realizing that the cooperation of the laity would be crucial, sent strongly worded messages to laymen and laywomen, reminding them that they were the front line of the church's mission in society and that, wherever they found themselves, they must strive to "consecrate the world itself to God." But events under way in the United States and other affluent countries would make it harder than ever for such messages to get through. The breakdown in sexual mores, the rise in family disruption, and the massive entry of mothers of young children into the labor force amounted to an enormous social experiment, an unprecedented demographic revolution for which neither the church nor the affected societies were prepared.

In those turbulent years, pressures intensified for Catholics to treat their religion as an entirely private matter and to adopt a pick-and-choose approach to doctrine. Many of their *habladors*—theologians, religious educators, and clergy—succumbed to the same temptations. In that context, it was not only difficult for the strong demands of Vatican II to be heard, but the messages that did get through were often scrambled. In an important sense, all the most divisive controversies of the postconciliar years were about how far Catholics could go in adapting to the prevailing culture while remaining Catholic.

Though American society was rapidly becoming more secular, certain cultural elements of Protestantism remained as strong as or stronger than ever: radical individualism, intolerance for dissent (redirected toward dissent from the secular dogmas that replaced Christianity in the belief systems of many), and an abiding hostility to Catholicism. For the upwardly mobile Catholic, assimilation into that culture thus meant acquiescing in anti-Catholicism to a degree that would have astonished our immigrant ancestors. But that's what all too many of us did. In the 1970s, Andrew Greeley observed that "of all the minority groups in this country, Catholics are the least concerned about their own rights and the least conscious of the persistent and systematic discrimination against them in the upper reaches of the corporate and intellectual worlds."

In this observation, as in his early warnings about child abuse and the growth of a homosexual subculture among the clergy, Fr. Greeley was on the mark. I regret to say that I was a case in point until my consciousness was raised by my Jewish husband. In the 1970s, when I was teaching at Boston College Law School, someone took down all the crucifixes from the walls one summer. Though the majority of the faculty at the time was Catholic and the dean was a Jesuit priest, not one of us entered a protest. When I told my husband, he was shocked. He said, "What's the matter with you Catholics? There would be an uproar if anyone did something like that with Jewish symbols. Why do Catholics put up with that kind of thing?" That was a turning point for me. I began to wonder: Why *do* we Catholics put up with that sort of thing? Why did we get so careless about the faith for which our ancestors made so many sacrifices?

In many cases, the answer lies simply in the desire to get ahead and be accepted. But for most Catholics of the American diaspora, I believe the problem is deeper: they no longer know how to talk about what they believe or why they believe it. The people-called-together has lost its sense of who it is and what it was called to do.

And it seems to have lost a lot of mail as well. How many laypeople, one wonders, have read any of the letters that popes have addressed to them over the years? For that matter, how many Catholics can give a sensible account of basic church teachings on matters as close to them as the Eucharist and human sexuality, let alone the lay apostolate? If few can do so, it is not for lack of communications from Rome. Building on *Rerum Novarum* and *Quadragesimo Anno,* the fathers of Vatican II reminded the lay faithful that it was their particular responsibility "to evangelize the various sectors of family, social, professional, cultural, and political life."

These have been constant themes of Pope John Paul II. In *Sollicitudo Rei Socialis,* to take just one example, he renewed the call to the social apostolate, emphasizing "the preeminent role" of the laity in protecting the dignity of the person and asking both "men and women . . . to be convinced of . . . each one's individual responsibility, and to implement—by the way they live as individuals and as families, by the use of their resources, by their civic activity, by contributing to economic and political decisions, and by personal commitment to national and international undertakings—the measures inspired by solidarity and love of preference for the poor."

He spelled out the implications of the lay vocation for contemporary Americans with great clarity in Baltimore in 1995: "Sometimes witnessing to Christ will mean drawing out of a culture the full meaning of its noblest intentions. . . . At other times, witnessing to Christ means challenging that culture, especially when the truth about the human person is under assault."

Now that the "sleeping giant" is beginning to show signs of regaining Catholic consciousness, the church is going to have to reckon with the fact that the most highly educated laity in its history has forgotten a great deal about where it came from. Meanwhile, as with any emerging mass movement, activists with definite ideas about where they would like it to go are eager to capture the giant's strength for their own purposes. In recent months, American Catholics have heard vague but strident calls for "structural reform," for lay "empowerment," and for more lay participation in the church's internal "decision making." Scott Appleby, for example, told the American bishops in Dallas, "I do not exaggerate by saying that the future of the church in this country depends upon your sharing authority with the laity." (See "The Church at Risk," p.19)

There has also been much talk about the need for a more independent American Catholic Church. "Let Rome be Rome," said Appleby. Then there is Governor Frank Keating, chosen by the bishops to head their National Review Board, who proclaimed, astonishingly, at his first press conference that, with respect to the role of the laity, "Martin Luther was right." Voice of the Faithful, an organization formed in 2002 by Boston suburbanites, states as its mission: "To provide a prayerful voice, attentive to the spirit, through which the faithful can actively participate in the governance and guidance of the Catholic Church." (One has to wonder just what spirits had been consulted when a leader of that group boasted excitedly to the *Boston Globe* that "the mainstream Catholics, all sixty-four million of them," were speaking through Voice of the Faithful's convention this past July.)

There is nary a sign, thus far, that these spokespersons have a sense of the main job the Gospels tell Christians they were placed on earth to do. Even the late Cardinal Basil Hume, hardly a reactionary in church matters, took pains to caution an earlier reform-minded group, the Catholic Common Ground Initiative, against "the danger of concentrating too much on the life within the Church." "I suspect," he said, "that it is a trick of the Devil to divert good people from the task of evangelization by embroiling them in endless controversial issues to the neglect of the Church's essential role, which is mission."

By leaving evangelization and the social apostolate out of the picture, many lay spokespersons are promoting some pretty basic misunderstandings: that the best way for the laity to be active is in terms of ecclesial governance; that the church and her structures are to be equated with public agencies or private corporations; that she and her ministers are to be regarded with mistrust; and that she stands in need of supervision by secular reformers. If those attitudes take hold, they will make it very difficult for the church to move forward through the present crisis without compromising either her teachings or her constitutionally protected freedom to carry out her mission.

Much of that careless talk simply reflects the fact that, with the decline of Catholic institutions, the actual experience of the lay apostolate has disappeared from the lives of most Catholics—along with the practical understanding of complementarity among the roles of the different members of the mystical body of Christ. It is only common sense that most of us laypeople are best equipped to fulfill our vocations primarily in the places where we live and work. It is because we are present in all the secular occupations that the Vatican II fathers emphasized our "special task" to take a more active part, according to our talents and knowledge, in the explanation and defense of Christian principles and in the application of them to the problems of our times. John Paul II elaborated on that theme in *Christifideles Laici,* pointing out that this will be possible in secularized societies only "if the lay faithful will know how to overcome in themselves the separation of the Gospel from life, to again take up in their daily activities in family, work, and society an integrated approach to life that is fully brought about by the inspiration and strength of the Gospel." Those are the main messages of all those letters that most of us have not read or answered. And those are the messages that are notably absent from the statements of spokespersons for the lay groups that have formed over the past few months.

As memories of the lived experience of the lay apostolate faded, the lay ministry expanded in the post-Vatican II years. It is not surprising, therefore, that many Catholics came to believe that the principal way to be active as Catholics was to participate in the internal life of the church. Those who began clamoring for more such participation in 2002 seem unaware that they are battering on an open door. The church has long been beseeching laymen and laywomen to come forward and assume positions at all levels. No one should complain, however, if bishops and priests are reluctant to give posts of responsibility to dissenters who want to use such positions to change basic church teachings. No good shepherd will invite wolves to look after his flock.

Needless to say, the church will need to undertake far-reaching reforms in order to move beyond the present crisis, and many of the recent calls for reform are coming from well-intentioned men and women. Most Catholics are deeply and rightly concerned about the recent revelations of clerical sexual abuse; they want to do something about the havoc wreaked by unfaithful priests, and they are grasping at the slogans that are in the air. But slogans about "structural reform" and "power sharing" did not come from nowhere. Aging members of the generation of failed theories—political, economic, and sexual—have seized on the current crisis as their last opportunity to transform American Catholicism into something more compatible with the spirit of the age of their youth. It is, as Michael Novak puts it, their last chance to rush the wall.

Southern writers such as Flannery O'Connor and Walker Percy saw where those warped visions could lead American Christianity long before most of the rest of us did. The antihero of O'Connor's *Wise Blood* sets himself up as a preacher of the Church of Christ Without Christ. Percy's 1971 novel, *Love in the Ruins,* is set in some not-too-distant future when the American Catholic Church has split into three pieces: the patriotic Catholic Church, with headquarters in Cicero, Illinois, where "The Star-Spangled Banner" is played at the elevation of the Host; the Dutch Reformed Catholic Church, founded by several priests and nuns who left to get married; and "the Roman Catholic remnant, a tiny scattered flock with no place to go." Happily, matters have not reached that point, but it is noteworthy that the two most salient themes of self-appointed lay spokespersons during the 2002 crisis have been in those directions: the desire for a more American church free of hierarchical authority, and the desire for a do-it-yourself magisterium free of hard teachings regarding sex and marriage.

Meanwhile, like Paul of old, John Paul II keeps sending those pesky letters reminding those whom he generously calls the faithful that Christians must not conform to the spirit of the age but must seek to do what is good, pleasing, and perfect in the sight of God. For the umpteenth time, he explains that "it is not a matter of inventing a 'new program.' The program already exists: it is the plan found in the Gospel and in the living Tradition; it is the same as ever." One might think those messages would at least be picked up and amplified by those Catholics whose profession it is to figure out how to mediate the truths that are "ever ancient and ever new" under changing social conditions. But the fact is that far too many American Catholic theologians, trained in nondenominational divinity schools, have received little grounding in their own tradition. Far too many religious-education materials are infused with the anger and disappointments of former priests and sisters who went to work in religious publishing because their training suited them for little else. And far too many bishops and priests have ceased to preach the word of God in its unexpurgated fullness, including the teachings that are most difficult to follow in a hedonistic and materialistic society.

Derelictions on the part of so many *habladors* have left far too many parents poorly equipped to contend with powerful competitors for the souls of their children—the aggressively secular government schools and an entertainment industry that revels in debasing everything Catholic. I do not mean to suggest that failures of theologians, religious educators, bishops, and priests excuse the lapses of the laity. What I do mean to suggest is that we are in the midst of a full-blown formation crisis.

Fr. Richard John Neuhaus has said that the crisis of the Catholic Church in 2002 is threefold: fidelity, fidelity, and fidelity. He is right to stress that lack of fidelity has brought the church in America to a sorry pass. But it also needs to be said that we are paying the price for another three-dimensional disaster: formation, formation, and formation (formation of our theologians, of our religious educators, and thus of parents).

The wordsmiths of the culture of death have been quick to exploit that weakness in what has consistently been their most feared and powerful enemy. Thirty or so years ago, they came up with one of the most insidious slogans ever invented: "Personally, I'm opposed to (fill in the blank), but I can't impose my opinions on others." That slogan was the moral anesthesia they offered to people who were troubled about moral decline but who did not know quite how to express their views, especially in public settings. Only in recent years have some Catholics, Protestants, and Jews stepped forward to point out that when citizens in a democratic republic advance religiously grounded moral viewpoints in the public square, they are not imposing anything on anyone. They are proposing. That is what is supposed to happen in our form of government—citizens propose, they give reasons, they deliberate, they vote. It is a sinister doctrine that would silence only those moral viewpoints that are religiously based. But the anesthesia was very effective in silencing the witness of countless good men and women. And of course the slogan was a bonanza for cowardly and unprincipled politicians.

At this point, a person aware that faith illiteracy has always been common might ask, "What's so urgent about formation now?" The answer is that poor formation presents a special danger in a society like ours, where Catholics have lost most of their old support networks and where education in other areas is relatively advanced. If religious education falls short of the general level of secular education, Christians run into trouble defending their beliefs—even to themselves. They are apt to feel helpless when they come up against the secularism and relativism that are so pervasive in the general culture.

It is ironic, given their rich intellectual heritage, that so many Catholics feel unable to respond even to the simplistic forms of secular fundamentalism that are prevalent among America's semiskilled knowledge class. Traditionally, it has been one of the glories of their faith that Catholics can give reasons for the moral positions they hold—reasons that are accessible to all men and women of goodwill, of other faiths or of no faith. Long ago, St. Thomas Aquinas wrote: "Instruct those who are listening so that they will be brought to an understanding of the truth envisaged. Here one must rely on arguments which probe the root of truth and make people know how what is said is true; otherwise, if the master decides a question simply by using sheer authorities, the hearer will . . . acquire no knowledge or understanding and will go away empty."

St. Thomas inspired Bartolomé de Las Casas, who denounced slavery and proclaimed the full humanity of aboriginal peoples in the sixteenth century without direct reliance on Revelation. And Princeton's Robert George does the same today in his philosophical defense of human life from conception to natural death. Recently, Dr. John Haas, the president of the National Catholic Bioethics Center, met with a well-known scientist who is engaged in human cloning. In the course of that meeting, the researcher told Dr. Haas that he had been raised an evangelical Protestant but that at a certain point "I knew I had to make a choice between religion and science, and I chose science." Dr. Haas's response, of course, was "But you don't have to choose," and, like the good evangelist that he is, he began to expound the teaching of *Fides et Ratio*. A meeting that was supposed to last thirty minutes went on for hours.

John Paul II urges Catholics to emulate such examples when he says in *Novo Millennio Ineunte*: "For Christian witness to be effective, especially in . . . delicate and controversial areas, it is important that special efforts be made to explain properly the reasons for the Church's position, stressing that it is not a case of imposing on nonbelievers a vision based on faith, but of interpreting and defending the values rooted in the very nature of the human person."

To explain the reasons, however, means that one must know the reasons. "Be not afraid" does not mean "Be not prepared."

The time is overdue for Catholics (not only in America) to recognize that we have neglected our stewardship duties toward the intellectual heritage that we hold in trust for future generations. The question of why we have failed to keep that tradition abreast of the best human and natural science of our times—as St. Thomas did in his day—would be a subject for another occasion. Suffice it to note here that, in the twentieth century, that was the project of Bernard Lonergan and others, but the job has had few takers. Andrew Greeley's diagnosis is harsh: "American Catholicism," he says, "did not try intellectualism and find it wanting; it rather found intellectualism hard and decided not to try it."

Perhaps Greeley is too severe, but it is hard to disagree with theologian Frederick Lawrence when he says that "the Church's current activity in the educational sphere is not making sufficiently manifest how the basic thrust of Catholic Christianity is in harmony with full-fledged intellectualism, let alone that intellectual life is integral to the Church's mission." Lawrence goes on to say, "The Church today needs to proclaim loud and clear that understanding the natural order of the cosmos in the human and subhuman sciences, and in philosophy and theology, is part of appreciating God's cosmic Word expressed in creation. It is part and parcel of the fullness of the Catholic mind and heart."

American Catholics need to rededicate themselves to the intellectual apostolate, not only for the sake of the church's mission, but also for the sake of a country that has become dangerously careless about the moral foundations on which our freedoms depend. Tocqueville was right that Catholicism can be good for American democracy, but that can only happen if Catholicism is true to itself.

Is it possible that the scandal-induced surge of lay activity in 2002 foreshadows a season of authentic reform and renewal? If one is hopeful, one can discern here and there some encouraging signs. A number of newly formed lay associations, for example, are said to be forming study groups to read church documents, encyclicals, and the *Catechism*. The most promising sign of better times ahead, however, is the growing generation of unapologetically Catholic young people, including many young priests, who have been inspired by the heroic life and teachings of John Paul II.

Meanwhile, the world as we know it is still passing away. The demographic landscape of the United States is once again being transformed by immigration, this time mainly from the south. The vast majority of these newcomers have been formed in the Catholic cultures of Central and South America and the Caribbean. True, many of them have lost their story, but even so, they tend to have a Catholic way of imagining the real, of looking at the human person and society. At present rates, the United States will soon be the country with the third-largest Catholic population in the world, after Brazil and Mexico. In the spring of 2002, while members of Boston's Voice of the Faithful were debating about church finances and governance, Boston's Latino Catholics were holding prayer vigils to affirm the solidarity of all the members of the mystical body of Christ—men and women, rich and poor, clergy and laity, and, yes, victims and abusers.

Wherever the sons and daughters of the American Catholic diaspora are to be found, one thing is certain. The members of the people-called-together are searching for the stories that will help them make sense of their lives. The woman on the bus who pores over the astrological chart in the morning paper is looking for meaning. The professor worshiping this or that ideological idol is looking for a creed to live by and for. The opinion polls telling us that most Americans believe the country is in a moral decline yet do not feel they can "impose" their morality on others testify to the confusion that afflicts good people in times when "the best lack all conviction, while the worst are full of passionate intensity."

What if the scattered Catholic faithful were to remember and embrace the heritage that is rightly theirs? What if they were to rediscover the newness of their faith and its power to judge the prevailing culture? What an awakening that would be for the sleeping giant! As John Paul II likes to tell young people, "If you are what you should be—that is, if you live Christianity without compromise—you will set the world ablaze!"

Is it fanciful to think that the people-called-together could rediscover the dynamic newness of its faith in its dispersed condition? Members of the church's great lay organizations around the world do not think so. Even as mobility has sapped the vitality of many parishes, there has been a great upsurge— mostly outside the United States thus far—in lay associations, formation programs, and ecclesial movements. These groups, so varied in their charisms, so rich in storytellers, are providing a way for Catholics to stay in touch with one another and with their tradition under diaspora conditions. John Paul II has recognized the remarkable accomplishments of these groups in the area of formation and has urged his brother bishops and priests to take full advantage of the potential they afford for personal and ecclesial renewal.

Until recently, I, like most American Catholics, was relatively unaware of the extent and variety of these movements. It was only through serving on the Pontifical Council for the Laity that I came to know groups like Communion and Liberation, the Community of Sant'Egidio, Focolare, the NeoCatechumenate Way, Opus Dei, and Regnum Christi and became acquainted with many of their leaders and members. What a contrast between these groups that work in harmony with the church and organizations that define their aims in

terms of power! It is no surprise that the more faithful and
vibrant the great lay organizations are, the more they are vili-
fied by dissenters and anti-Catholics. But attacks do not seem
to trouble them, for they know who they are and where they
are going.

Finally, one of the great blessings of having a papacy and
a magisterium is that they help ensure that the story of the
people-called-together will be preserved, even in the most
trying times. In Vargas Llosa's *Storyteller,* an outsider comes
to the dispersed Machiguengas, a man who loves the people-
who-walk and their stories so much that he becomes their
hablador. He is often on the road, traveling from family to
family, bringing news from one place to the next, "reminding
each member of the tribe that the others are alive, that despite
the great distances that [separate] them, they still [form] a
community, [share] a tradition and beliefs, ancestors, misfor-
tunes, and joys." Among the many reasons to rejoice in the
long pontificate of John Paul II is that, like the greatest of
habladors, he has kept the story of his people radiantly alive,
carrying it to every corner of the earth in one of humanity's
darkest times.

Please Touch

Gregory Wolfe

from *Image*

Having grown up in what I would call a rather Waspy milieu
in New York's Upper East Side, my youthful aesthetic sensi-
bility was, to some extent, predetermined. My mother took
me to see the classics of art history at the Metropolitan, but
she also took me to the Museum of Modern Art and the
Guggenheim. I was surrounded by the austere simplicity of
high modernism; that slowly ascending spiral of Frank Lloyd
Wright's Guggenheim was as much a part of my mental landscape as it was of the cityscape of my neighborhood.

In those childhood years, we attended a Christian Science
church, so my religious aesthetic was similarly shaped by a
sort of minimalist neoclassicism. When we switched to the
Congregational Church in my adolescence, I could detect no
real change in architecture and only a modest expansion of
liturgical possibilities.

Even in my college years, when I had become an
Episcopalian and an ardent believer in the centrality of sign
and sacrament for the life of faith, I tended to like the spare-
ness of stone cathedrals, with their gray verticality. It was only
when I went to a cathedral in England that I learned that

medieval stone churches were painted in vivid colors, that they were, in fact, a riot of sensory stimulation. This was a blow, but it made me realize that I had treated Gothic stone more as a protomodernist achievement than the sensual, organic thing it really was. So I began to notice other architectural styles, including the Baroque, and to actually pay attention to statuary, the depiction of saints and angels.

My aesthetic was beginning to yield, and with it my faith. When I was a child, my spirituality, echoing the architecture around me, seemed to consist of ethical simplicity, the recollection of ancient but enduring ideas—something to be experienced in the head rather than the heart. Perhaps one of the legacies of my early immersion in Christian Science was a feeling that the human body was something of an embarrassment, if not a prison. But I wasn't satisfied with this. I didn't want to be a ghost in my own flesh.

So began a journey that eventually led me into the Roman Catholic Church. Not surprisingly, the Virgin Mary did not play a large role in my religious search. I found Marian kitsch—the gaudy popular Catholic representations of Mary, in plastic and plaster—so alien and off-putting that I wondered if I could ever become a coreligionist with the people who made and venerated such things. Deep cultural programming told me that the folks who came up to these figures—leaving flowers at their feet, hanging rosaries on the outstretched hand of the Christ child, touching the base of the elevated statues so that the paint rubbed off the toes of the Virgin—were more like primitive pantheists than civilized believers.

It took me years to realize that what kept me away from Mary was not merely a disdain for popular Catholic devotion but my own abstracted and overly cerebral faith. A slowly developing hunger for the sacraments—for the grace of God to be not merely understood or even felt but actually *touched,* in the common stuff of life, including bread, wine, water, and oil—slowly brought me closer to Mary. For she was the human vessel whose womb and breasts and arms and tear ducts were the necessary conduits through which the Son of God became the Son of man. I no longer felt satisfied thinking about God; I needed to feel his touch on my tongue.

And then I looked again at all those representations of Mary, from hideously bejeweled plastic dolls to numinously beautiful alabaster statues, and I could see one message conveyed over and over again. As our Lady holds the Child, simultaneously protecting him and presenting him to the world that would crucify him, she seems to say to us: *Please touch.*

Representations of Mary seem to revel in paradox: as Virgin she is untouched, but as mother she is constantly touching others. In all those paintings of the Annunciation, Mary is depicted as praying or reading at the moment she receives the message from Gabriel, but even when she is in contemplation her body language is eloquent—she recoils and assents in one complicated gesture. At the foot of the cross she receives her Son into her arms once more. As refuge of sinners, she spreads her mantle around gathered humanity, protecting and consoling.

This was brought home to me once when I was praying in El Santuario de Chimayo, the New Mexican chapel that has become known as the Lourdes of America. Chimayo is the place where the Virgin appeared to a local farmer and answered his prayer by blessing the barren earth and making it fecund. This, too, is about touch, for the earth is the skin of the world.

As I was praying and daydreaming, a Hispanic woman came toward the front of the chapel. She paid no attention to the magnificent nineteenth-century painted *reredos* in the Spanish colonial style but approached a small, mass-produced plaster statue of the Virgin. Wracked by sobs and streaming tears, the woman was inconsolable. It was impossible to tell what she mourned. But over the next ten minutes she drew close to the statue and touched it with her outstretched fingertips, with a strange combination of reticence and compulsion. She touched and then withdrew a number of times in an agonized dance that somehow seemed to me at that moment to be steps taken from the choreography of heaven. Eventually a friend guided her out of the sanctuary. I couldn't be sure, but I thought that she had experienced some small measure of consolation, that some exchange had taken place in that dance, that hesitant, confident touching of the mother.

Twenty-Five Years: The Papacy of John Paul II

John L. Allen Jr.

from *National Catholic Reporter*

Is John Paul II liberal or conservative? Is he pro- or anti-Western? Is he the liberator of the peoples behind the iron curtain, or someone many women regard as an obstacle to their emancipation? Is he the pope who gave away his episcopal ring in a Brazilian shantytown to express the church's solidarity with the poor, or the pope who broke the back of liberation theology? Is he the pope who apologized for Galileo and Jan Hus, or the pope who cracked down on Hans Küng and Charles Curran? Is he the pope who visited the Rome synagogue and the Western Wall, or the pope who beatified Pius IX? Is he the pope who gave the archbishop of Canterbury a gold pectoral cross, a symbol of episcopal authority, or is he the pope who approved a document elevating to quasi-infallible status the teaching that Anglican ordinations are invalid?

The truth is that this pope is all of the above.

No public figure of the twentieth century, and perhaps few ever, defies easy categorization quite like Pope John Paul II.

His pontificate marked its twenty-fifth anniversary on October 16, 2003, and over that quarter century, John Paul has stood at the center of all of the most important religious, political, and cultural tensions of his time. Biographer Jonathan Kwitny once called Karol Wojtyla the "man of the century," not necessarily because he was the twentieth century's greatest man but because all of the century's historical dramas cut across his own life story. Perhaps it's that complexity that makes John Paul's worldview maddeningly difficult to pin down from the standpoint of either partisan politics or the usual philosophical systems.

Nietzsche once said that great men should be beyond good and evil—an option clearly not available to a pope. Yet there is a sense in which a pope has to be beyond the confines of strict logic, for the sake of keeping his massive worldwide community of faith in equilibrium. John XXIII once put the point this way: "I have to be pope both for those with their foot on the gas and those with their foot on the brake."

On this rare milestone—only two other popes have reigned twenty-five years or more, Leo XIII and Pius IX, both in the nineteenth century—any attempt to spell out the significance and contributions of John Paul's pontificate from a single angle of vision is thus destined to be an exercise in selective perception. Instead, we'll consider how his papacy looks from multiple points of view: of Jews, theologians in Europe and North America, Arab Christians, educated Catholic women, Catholic social activists in Latin America, Catholics of the Eastern churches, traditionally minded Catholics, and moderate American bishops.

As Einstein theorized about place and time, so too John Paul's legacy is, in important respects, relative to where one stands.

Jews

As a Pole coming of age in the 1930s, Karol Wojtyla watched the Nazi assault against European Jewry unfold. He grew up in a mixed Christian-Jewish community in Wadowice, and his best friend was a young Jew named Jerzy Kluger. In just one among a thousand signs of John Paul's special affinity to Jews, he is the first pope ever to speak Yiddish. Polish Jews remember Archbishop Karol Wojtyla with fondness; during the pope's 2002 trip to Poland, a leader of Kraków's Jewish community described how Wojtyla had "reached out a blessing hand to us."

That life experience has made him a historic force as far as Jewish relations are concerned. In 1986, John Paul became the first pope since the age of St. Peter to set foot inside a Jewish place of worship, visiting the Rome synagogue. In 2000, John Paul visited Jerusalem's Western Wall, also known as the Wailing Wall for its sad Jewish history, leaving behind a handwritten note expressing regret for centuries of Christian anti-Semitism. "We are deeply saddened by the behavior of those who in the course of history have caused these children of yours to suffer and, asking your forgiveness, we wish to commit ourselves to genuine brotherhood with the people of the Covenant," it read.

The transformation in Jewish-Christian relations has played itself out in practical ways in dialogues, exchanges, and joint service projects. The climate is sufficiently new that on September 11, 2000, more than 150 rabbis and Jewish university professors signed a public statement called "*Dabru Emet:* A Jewish Statement on Christians and Christianity," asserting that "it is time for Jews to learn about the efforts of Christians to honor Judaism."

Indeed, John Paul has been so consequential that influential Jewish leaders around the world are taking an unusual interest in the politics of the papal transition, worried that his successor will not have the same existential "feel" for Jewish-Christian relations.

Not every American Jew, however, is quite so impressed.

The decision to beatify Pius IX, the pope who kidnapped a Jewish child in Bologna and who put Rome's Jews back in their ghetto, is one serious question mark. Another is John Paul's decision not to respond when President Bashar al-Assad, in the course of welcoming the pope to Syria in May 2001, said that Jews had killed Christ and tried to kill Muhammad.

Debate over the possible beatification of Pius XII, the canonization of Edith Stein, the implosion of a mixed commission of Jewish and Catholic scholars to deal with the Vatican archives, and lingering bitterness over a Carmelite convent at Auschwitz all cloud the relationship. There are also less significant disappointments, such as the choice to visit the Soviet-era memorial to all the victims of fascism at Babi Yar during the 2001 trip to Ukraine rather than the specifically Jewish monument a few hundred meters away.

Moreover, the pope's personal example has only gone so far, and perhaps could only go so far, in undoing ancient prejudices. This is true even within the Holy See, where the working assumption of an enmity between Jews and Christians is still alive in some quarters. This came into view during the American clergy sex-abuse crisis, for example, when some Vatican officials quietly whispered that the attacks in the U.S. press represented the Jewish-dominated media's payback for the church's support of the Palestinians.

Yet even granting these shadows, many Jews would probably concur with Rabbi Michael Kogan of Montclair State University in New Jersey.

"This pope is the best pope the Jews ever had," Kogan told the *National Catholic Reporter*. "Some Catholics may not like

him, but as far as we're concerned, he's great. He is determined that the church will enter the twenty-first century free
of anti-Semitism."

Theologians in Europe and North America

If you put three Catholic theologians in a room, you'll have
four opinions, so to pretend there is anything like a consensus
view of John Paul's pontificate would be nonsense. On the
other hand, a survey of the theological community in Europe
and North America would probably reveal majorities on the
following points:

- The relationship between the magisterium, meaning the
  Vatican and the bishops, and the theological guild today
  is experienced as more adversarial than collaborative.
- Many theologians avoid certain areas of inquiry these
  days, such as sexual ethics and religious pluralism, on
  the grounds that it's not "safe" to speak or publish
  creative ideas on these topics.
- Many Catholic academics believe there has been a
  blurring of the lines between theology and catechesis,
  or apologetics, with the Vatican seeming to want theologians to act more like catechists, simply repeating
  formulas rather than critically examining them.
- Efforts to police orthodoxy have put many theologians in the awkward position of downplaying or cen-
  soring their own convictions about matters such as
  birth control or women in the church.

Whether these impressions are right or wrong, fair or
unfair is another matter, but they do represent what many

professional Catholic theologians, teaching at Catholic institutions and understanding themselves as loyal to the church, think.

Cardinal Joseph Ratzinger, John Paul's top doctrinal aide, has scoffed at suggestions of an oppressive climate within the church, observing that the actual number of theologians who have gone through his office's full disciplinary process is low, perhaps as few as a baker's dozen. But this overlooks the fact that many of these targets have been carefully chosen as symbols of whole trajectories in Catholic thought—Charles Curran for sexual ethics, Leonardo Boff for liberation theology, Jacques Dupuis and Roger Haight for religious pluralism.

Of course, not every Catholic theologian analyzes John Paul's pontificate in these terms. Many are grateful to the pope for what they see as vigorous intellectual leadership, especially in well-received encyclicals such as *Veritatis Splendor* in 1993 and *Fides et Ratio* in 1998. Many would also agree with the essential argument of the Congregation for the Doctrine of the Faith's 1990 "Instruction on the Ecclesial Vocation of the Theologian," that "the freedom proper to theological research is exercised within the church's faith."

Perhaps what one can say about John Paul and theologians is that his determination to draw lines in the sand has cheered those who find themselves within the boundaries and alienated many who feel the lines have been wrongly drawn.

Arab Christians

Of the world's 1.5 billion Christians, only 14 million or so live across the Arab world, with the largest concentrations in Egypt, Lebanon, and Iraq. Yet these Christian populations exercise a disproportionate hold on the imagination of the Christian world, because they are the caretakers of Christianity's holiest

sites, and because they cling tenaciously to an increasingly per-
ilous future.

The clearest confirmation of the threat to Arab Christianity
is the ongoing shrinkage of these communities, as growing
numbers of frightened Christians pull up stakes and leave. Today
more Christians born in Jerusalem live in Sydney, Australia,
than in the city of their birth. More Christians from Beit Jala, a
traditionally Christian town near Bethlehem, now reside in
Belize in Central America than are left in Beit Jala itself. In
Bethlehem, the city of Christ's birth, the Christian population
was reduced from a 60 percent majority in 1990 to a 20 percent minority in 2001, meaning some twenty-three thousand
people left the region. In Iraq, the situation is similar. Some two
hundred thousand Christians have left since the first Gulf War.
At the start of 1991, the Catholic population of Baghdad was
more than five hundred thousand. Today, Catholics number
about 175,000. "It's like a biblical exodus," one Vatican official
told the *National Catholic Reporter* in February 2002.

No attempt to understand the deep affection of most Arab
Christians for John Paul II can ignore this reality.

In fact, John Paul's outreach to Jews has been matched
almost pace-for-pace by his efforts with Muslims. He was not
just the first pope to visit a synagogue, but also the first pope
to enter a mosque, visiting the Grand Mosque of Omayyad in
Damascus in May 2001. While he has pushed forward with
Jewish-Christian dialogue, he has also met Muslims more than
sixty times, including visits to majority-Islamic nations such as
Egypt, Syria, and Morocco.

The same message that the pope is a friend of Islam was
the subtext to John Paul's stern moral opposition to the U.S.-
led war in Iraq. Before fighting broke out, observers feared
that Arab Christians would be targeted for anti-Western back-
lash. Yet in the most intense periods of the conflict, only a
handful of such cases occurred. Most observers credit the

result to John Paul's stance, since it allowed the "Islamic street" to distinguish between the West, Christianity, and the Bush administration.

All these gestures have helped reassure Muslim public opinion that one can be both Arab and Christian, that the latter does not mean disloyalty to the former.

Hence for Arab Christians, perhaps the force of John Paul's personality has not been enough to reverse the long-term threats facing their community, but his outreach to Islam has at least made their situation more tenable.

Educated Catholic Women

Perhaps John Paul's comparatively enlightened approach to women—appointing women as his spokespersons at international conferences, opposing discrimination against women in public policy—is the most one could reasonably expect from a Polish church leader of his generation and life experience.

Measured against the expectations of many educated Catholic women, however, especially in the developed world, the pope has often seemed a disappointment. Their sense of alienation can be profound. This includes some of the women who under other circumstances would be considered the church's most loyal base of support.

An anecdote about a disaster that almost was makes the point.

When John Paul II visited Toronto in June 2002 for World Youth Day, he spent most of his nights at Morrow Park, in a motherhouse and retirement home for the Sisters of St. Joseph. The nuns had turned their facility upside down to accommodate the pope and his entourage. Many were aged and infirm, and one even asked her spiritual director if it would be selfish to ask God to keep her alive long enough to meet the pope. Plans called for the superior of the community to greet John Paul in brief remarks at lunch, while the other sisters would join the lunch in the refectory along with the Canadian bishops and members of the papal party.

At the last minute, however, the nuns were told that they would not be taking part, and there would be no greeting. Local organizers scrambled to find out what had gone wrong, and eventually word came down from the pope's inner circle that no religious woman was to speak. The reason was fear that the nuns might deliver some sort of feminist statement, reflecting the memory of Sr. Theresa Kane, an American Mercy nun who in October 1979 publicly pleaded in front of John Paul that all ministries of the church be open to women.

In the end, the pope himself saved the day, agreeing immediately when an organizer asked whether he would like to meet the sisters. The point, however, is that the near miss illustrates the paranoia that can surround the "women's issue" on John Paul's watch.

Flash points include the United Nations Conference on Population and Development in Cairo in 1994 and the World Women's Conference in Beijing in 1995, both moments in which the Holy See challenged the agenda of international women's groups. Other tensions include a battle throughout the 1990s concerning "inclusive language," meaning non-gender-specific terminology in scriptural translations and liturgical texts, and the U.S. bishops' lengthy effort to produce a pastoral letter on women, eventually scuttled in the wake of repeated Vatican interventions.

Finally, the 1994 apostolic letter *Ordinatio Sacerdotalis* affirmed that the ban on women's ordination is a matter of divine revelation. The Congregation for the Doctrine of the Faith later said that this teaching has been "set forth infallibly" by the magisterium. While John Paul has argued that this teaching is about fidelity and not about power and that women have separate rather than inferior roles to play in the church, that line of argument has been unconvincing to many Catholics who think the real concern is maintenance of patriarchy. The failure of John Paul to move significant numbers of women into positions that do not require ordination, such as Vatican leadership posts, reinforces this impression.

Naturally, not every Catholic woman feels this way. Some believe that the pope, with his doctrine of male-female complementarity, as well as his defense of life and of the family, coupled with his fierce devotion to the Virgin Mary, has pointed the way to a more authentic "new feminism." Defenders also point out that the pope has appointed an unprecedented number of women to pontifical councils and academies.

In 1988, John Paul even published an encyclical letter on the dignity of women, titled *Mulieris Dignitatem,* which affirms the contemporary women's movement as a positive "sign of the times," though it also warns against the "masculinization" of women.

At the end of the day, however, even the staunchest defenders of John Paul tend to acknowledge that the Catholic Church has a problem with women. A bishops-sponsored survey of Australian Catholics in 1999 reached a conclusion that has parallels across much of the Catholic world, finding that a widespread sense of "pain, alienation, and often anger resulted from a strong sense of women's marginalization, struggle, disenfranchisement, powerlessness, irrelevance, and lack of acknowledgement in the church."

Whether the blame for this is to be placed on the pope, on aggressive feminism, or on some other combination of factors is in the eye of the beholder.

Catholic Social Activists in Latin America

John Paul has been a relentless critic of social injustice. Citations could be compounded almost indefinitely. In January 1999, for example, the pope issued his conclusion to the Synod for America, condemning "social sins" and the viciousness of neoliberalism.

Italian historian Andrea Riccardi, founder of the Community of Sant'Egidio recounts a conversation on July 22, 1979, in which the pope expressed his own view of the deficiencies of capitalism: "Look, I can surely say by now that I've got the antibodies to communism inside me. But when I think of consumer society, with all its tragedies, I wonder which of the two systems is better."

John Paul's relentless insistence on humanizing globalization has put the advocacy of social justice in the job description of church leaders. Under his guidance, a new generation of bishops has come of age across Latin America—Cardinals Oscar Andrés Rodríguez Maradiaga in Honduras, Jorge Mario Bergoglio in Argentina, and Cláudio Hummes in Brazil—a generation passionately committed to the struggle for justice.

At the same time, however, John Paul will forever be remembered in Latin America as the pope who gave a cold shoulder to Archbishop Oscar Romero of El Salvador, as the pope who authorized a crackdown on liberation theologians such as Leonardo Boff, and as the pope who publicly upbraided Jesuit Fr. Ernesto Cardenal for his political commitment.

Taken individually, each of these actions may be explicable given the circumstances and issues. Boff, for example, got into trouble not so much for his views on social matters as for his ecclesiology in the book *Church: Charism and Power*, which seemed to promote a kind of class struggle inside the church. Certainly few serious Christians could argue with Cardinal

Darío Castrillón Hoyos, who said of the most extreme versions of liberation theology, "When I see a church with a machine gun, I cannot see the crucified Christ in that church."

Moreover, John Paul's own attitude toward liberation theology was never wholly negative. In 1979, John Paul said he supported the idea of a theology of liberation but that it should not be tied exclusively to Latin America or to the sociologically poor. He quoted theologian Hans Urs von Balthasar to the effect that a Catholic theology must have a "universal radius." Later, he encouraged the drafting of a more positive document after the Congregation for the Doctrine of the Faith issued a harsh rebuke in 1984. The result, 1986's "Instruction on Christian Freedom and Liberation," for the first time in a magisterial document adopted the phrase "integral salvation" to describe the redemption won by Jesus Christ.

In a letter to Brazil's bishops in 1986, John Paul called liberation theology "not only opportune, but useful and necessary."

Collectively, however, the actions taken in the crackdown unleashed under John Paul created the impression that the Vatican had taken sides against Latin American Catholicism's most distinctive attempt to apply the Second Vatican Council.

Many Latin American social activists hence feel a deep ambivalence about John Paul. They approve much of his social teaching (while noting a certain incoherence between the fiercely anticapitalist *Sollicitudo Rei Socialis* and the more ambiguous *Centesimus Annus*) and his pastoral instincts. Yet they also know that he's the same pope who groomed Cardinal Alfonso López Trujillo of Colombia, who made a personal crusade out of the assault on liberation theology. John Paul has yet to advance the sainthood causes of any of the movement's martyrs, such as Romero, the six Jesuits and their housekeeper and her daughter killed at the University of Central

America in 1989, or the four American churchwomen (Ita Ford, Dorothy Kazel, Jean Donovan, and Maura Clarke) killed in El Salvador in December 1980.

Activists may thus see John Paul's papacy as a glass half full, emphasizing his strong prophetic language and doctrinal progress, or half empty, focusing on the disciplinary moves and his aversion to liberation theology's heroes.

Catholics of the Eastern Churches

Arguably few Catholic communities in the twentieth century suffered more for their fidelity than Eastern Catholics, whose churches were forcibly dissolved under the Soviets and whose clergy were generally given the option of becoming Orthodox priests or going to jail. The stories sometimes defy belief. One Greek Catholic priest in Ukraine was crucified upside down on a prison wall for his refusal to cut ties with Rome; another was boiled alive in a vat of oil.

This is the stuff of early Christian martyrologies, with the difference that these events happened just fifty years ago.

There are twenty-one Eastern churches in communion with Rome, and typically they have two overarching preoccupations. The first is a worry that amid the massive worldwide Latin rite, their distinctive identity will be lost. The second is the question of relations with the Orthodox traditions out of which most emerged. On both points, John Paul II has been arguably the most sensitive pope in history.

First, he has clearly made the preservation of Eastern traditions a priority of his pontificate, pushing through a new edition of the Code of Canon Law for Eastern Churches and calling repeatedly for Catholicism to "breathe with both lungs," East and West. He has visited virtually every nation in which an Eastern Catholic church community is found, meeting with their leaders and elevating their social profile.

In October 2001, John Paul approved a Vatican ruling that recognized the legitimacy of the eucharistic prayer used by the Assyrian Church of the East, the Orthodox companion to the Chaldean Catholic Church, even though it lacks an institution narrative—traditionally considered the essential element for valid eucharistic consecration. The ruling was considered stunning by many experts and a further sign of the pope's determination that Eastern rites and traditions be shown respect.

Second, John Paul, the first Slavic pope, has engaged in a historic campaign of rapprochement with the Orthodox. He has a long list of breakthroughs to show for the effort, including a Christological agreement with Oriental Orthodox churches in 1994 declaring the old Monophysite controversies resolved; well-received trips to Greece, Romania, Georgia, and Bulgaria; and high-level exchanges with all the hierarchies of the fifteen autocephalous Orthodox churches.

In 1995's *Ut Unum Sint* ("That They May Be One"), John Paul offered to open a dialogue with the church's ecumenical partners about how the papacy might be restructured, a gesture intended above all for the Orthodox, for whom the papacy is the single towering practical and theological obstacle to greater unity. During his May 2001 trip to Greece, John Paul offered an apology to the Orthodox that seemed to dispel centuries of bad blood.

Despite that, Catholic-Orthodox relations have frequently hit a brick wall. In mid-September 2003, for example, Archbishop Jean-Louis Tauran, the Vatican's foreign minister, traveled to Georgia to sign a bilateral agreement that was scuttled at the last minute due to strong opposition from Orthodox nationalists, marching under the banner of "Georgia without the Vatican." The Russian Orthodox Church has for years denied John Paul his dream of a trip to Moscow, citing proselytism by Catholics in Russia and property disputes in western Ukraine.

Despite these tensions, however, most Eastern Catholics regard John Paul as a hero. Jesuit Fr. Robert Taft, an American expert on the Eastern churches, said there's no argument about the historical significance of John Paul's papacy from his point of view.

"On the issues I work on, he's been one of the best popes we've ever had," Taft said. "I understand why others might be more critical, but when it comes to my professional interests, he's terrific."

Catholic Traditionalists

Catholics who regret the abandonment of older liturgical practices or who worry about the doctrinal solidity of post–Vatican II church teaching find much to praise in John Paul II. They applaud the 1988 *Ecclesia Dei* indult that allowed the celebration of the pre–Vatican II Latin Mass with the permission of local bishops. They were heartened by the pope's willingness to draw lines in the sand against what they saw as clearly excessive theological dissent. They support John Paul's plain talk on issues of sexual morality and his capacity to denounce what he sees as a "culture of death."

At the same time, however, traditionalists also feel alienated from this pontificate in many important ways.

On liturgical matters, for example, they charge that the pope may be a reverent celebrant himself who says Mass in Latin every morning, but he has largely been content to let the post–Vatican II liturgical deconstruction unfold. He even appointed as his own master of ceremonies an Italian liturgist, Bishop Piero Marini, who was the private secretary of the man responsible for the conciliar liturgical reforms, Archbishop Annibale Bugnini.

Moreover, while John Paul's stands on abortion, birth control, and gay rights have cheered traditionalists, his stance on some doctrinal questions has been far less reassuring. His decision to call leaders of the world religions to Assisi three times to pray for peace (1986, 1993, and 2002) created worries about relativism, or the idea that one religion is as good as another, and syncretism, a blending of elements of different religions into one New Age pâté.

In general, the pope's ecumenical and interreligious outreach has led some traditionalists to charge him with "indifferentism," treating truth and error as if they're the same thing. This line of concern even led some conservative Catholics to criticize John Paul's 1992 beatification of Opus Dei founder Josemaria Escriva, since Escriva allowed non-Catholics and even non-Christians to sign up as "collaborators" of Opus Dei.

Italian writer Vittorio Messori coined a phrase to sum up this traditionalist critique of John Paul: "Strong on morals but weak on faith."

Conservatives also sometimes grumble that John Paul has indulged his own personal intellectual tastes too much in magisterial documents, replacing the scholasticism derived from Thomas Aquinas with a twentieth-century personalism that owes more to Edmund Husserl and Martin Heidegger.

John Paul's style has always rubbed some traditionalists, including some in the Vatican, the wrong way: too much travel, too many saints, too many spectacles in St. Peter's Square, too much face time on TV, too much emphasis on his personal devotion to Mary and previously obscure figures such as the Polish nun and visionary Faustina Kowalska.

Finally, some traditionalists say the pope's willingness to fight dissent has been far too episodic and inconsistent. Sure, Hans Küng lost his license to teach Catholic theology, but Fr. Richard McBrien is still happily ensconced at the University of Notre Dame, and with him a host of other liberal theologians. While the Congregation for the Doctrine of the Faith issues stern reminders on the ecclesial vocation of the theologian, bishops who challenge that position, such as Germans Karl Lehmann and Walter Kasper, even manage to become cardinals. A whole generation of church bureaucrats and pastoral workers remains in place despite indications of deep differences with at least certain elements of the *Catechism of the Catholic Church*.

After twenty-five years of John Paul's reign, therefore, traditional Catholics may admire the pope's moral stands, but at the same time they fear that his doctrinal, philosophical, and administrative leadership has been at best a mixed bag, and in some cases downright toxic.

Moderate American Bishops

Most bishops feel a tremendous admiration for John Paul II as a man of deep fidelity and obvious personal holiness. They watch him pour himself out in service and cannot help but be moved. Moreover, they know the affection he awakens in people, especially the young, and the moral esteem in which he is held even outside the Catholic Church.

At the same time, many American bishops feel reservations about some aspects of John Paul's pontificate, especially the way in which it seems to have operated at times on an adversarial model with respect to bishops and bishops' conferences. The symbol of this approach would be the 1998

document *Apostolos Suos,* which held that episcopal conferences had no right to teach on matters of faith and morals in
their own name.

Most Americans, along with a large chunk of the rest of the
Catholic world, regarded this as a classic exercise in raw power
politics. Faced with a wealthy, respected, and influential national
conference in the United States and equally impressive regional
conferences in Latin America and Asia, the Vatican wanted to cut
them off at the knees. Many American Catholics were proud of
the accomplishments of their bishops' conference in the 1980s,
with its well-received documents on the economy and on peace.
The idea that their bishops were being "punished" for such success was galling.

It should be understood, however, that seen through the eyes
of the Vatican, *Apostolos Suos* was designed to bolster, not compromise, the authority of individual bishops, ensuring that their
voice was not drowned out by an ecclesiastical bureaucracy.

More broadly, some American bishops worry that too many
decisions under John Paul have been reserved to Rome, violat-
ing the balance that should exist between unity and flexibility.
The long struggle to bring the translation of liturgical texts
into English under Roman control is one illustration.

Bishops also frequently complain that John Paul's advisers
listen too much to disgruntled Catholics who happen to
express a bias that is in favor in Rome rather than a serious
pastoral problem that requires an intervention.

Finally, many American bishops are disheartened by the
alienation and polarization that exist in the U.S. church
among so many classes—women, pastoral workers, theologians, activists. This is perhaps not the pope's fault, but obviously he has not figured out a solution, and the bitterness has
become far more intense in the wake of the American clergy
sex-abuse crisis.

"John Paul has been a great pope," one American bishop said in the summer of 2003. "But he's leaving behind a hell of a pile of unfinished business for the next guy."

Beyond Doctrine and Politics

One could go on considering other groups—African Catholics, for example, or young Catholics who have flocked to see John Paul as part of World Youth Day celebrations. But the point should be clear: this pope's legacy is complex, and even from a single vantage point, one can usually find both light and shadows.

So what can we say with certainty, not just from one or another point of view but in the absolute, about John Paul II, 264th successor of St. Peter, on the twenty-fifth anniversary of his election?

First, he *matters*. He changed the face of Europe, stopped a handful of wars and inveighed against others, traveled the equivalent of three and a half times to the moon, and has been seen in person by more human beings than anyone else in history. He has to be numbered among the titans of his time.

This pope is indeed a magnet for humanity, including the 4.5 to 5 million people in Manila in 1995 for World Youth Day and the 10 million in Mexico City in 1979. The only events that compare are the Hindu Kumbh Mela festival of January 2001, when ten million people bathed in the Ganges River over twenty-four hours, and the funeral of the Iranian Muslim leader Ayatollah Khomeini in June 1989, which drew three to ten million.

Second, one can say that precisely because John Paul matters, he also *divides*. He lives the title of the retreats he preached for Paul VI as archbishop of Kraków: a "sign of contradiction." Everyone has an opinion on John Paul II, which is perhaps the most convincing sign of his impact.

His twenty-five years in power have been a whirlwind of activity: 102 trips outside Italy, 474 saints, 1,314 beatifications, 14 encyclicals, and on and on . . . and the production continues. On the very day of his twenty-fifth anniversary, John Paul will release yet another apostolic constitution, this one the conclusion of the October 2001 Synod for Bishops. While all this activity has made the pope famous, it has also made him controversial. It has been a bruising, painful, polarizing pontificate, one of the reasons why some cardinals say his successor should perhaps be a quieter, less-dominating figure who doesn't tower over the scene in quite the same way.

Finally, one can say with confidence that Karol Wojtyla, deeper than his politics and beyond his early-twentieth-century Polish Catholic cultural formation, is a *Mensch*. He is a strong, intelligent, caring human being, someone whose integrity and dedication to duty represent a standard by which other leaders can be measured.

For one thing, John Paul is a selfless figure in a me-first world. Cardinal Roberto Tucci, who planned John Paul's voyages before retiring in 2001, once said he had briefed John Paul hundreds of times on the details for his various trips. Not once, Tucci said, did the pope ever ask where he was going to sleep, what he would eat or wear, or what his creature comforts would be. The same indifference to himself can be seen every time the pope steps—or today, is rolled—upon the public stage.

This is the key that unlocks why John Paul draws enormous crowds, even in places where his specific political or doctrinal stands may be unpopular. It's a rare ideologue for whom condoms or the Latin Mass represent ultimate concerns. Deeper than politics, either secular or ecclesiastical, lies the realm of personal integrity—goodness and holiness, the qualities we prize most in colleagues, family, and friends. A person may be liberal or conservative, avant-garde or traditional, but let him or her be decent, and most of the time that's enough.

This realm of *Menschlichkeit,* authentic humanity, is where John Paul's appeal comes from. For a pope of a hundred trips and a million words, perhaps the most important lesson he's offered is the coherence of his own life. When he urges Christians, in the words of Jesus, to "*duc in altum*"—to set off into the deep—it resonates even with those who seek very different shores.

As Hamlet said of his father, perhaps John Paul's admirers and critics together might be able to say of him: "He was a man. Take him for all in all, I shall not look upon his like again."

Not a Sparrow Falls

Paul Scanlon, OP

from *Treasures from the Poor in Spirit*

The tropical rain pounded the sixteenth-century church so hard it was nearly impossible for us to hear one another. My fellow Chiapas missionaries and I stepped outside, stood under the eaves, and chatted idly until we noticed a man standing in the cloister garden.

He had no umbrella, no rain gear. Apparently beaten down by more than the storm, he didn't move. I wish I could say I rushed over to help him, but I didn't.

My friend Sr. Mari stepped out into the rain and led him inside. She dried him off. Fluent in Tzeltal, she listened to his story.

His name was Manuel. His wife had just died, and he didn't know what to do or where to go. Sr. Mari said she would accompany him to the carpenter's shop and have a casket made.

That evening Sr. Mari and I, accompanied by Fr. Vincent, the pastor, headed out in the mission's truck to pick up the grieving widower and the coffin. We loaded the simple pine box into the truck bed, and Manuel and I climbed in beside it. By now the storm had passed through Ocosingo and was headed toward Guatemala, but the road was thick with mud as we drove off beyond the edge of town and past the last few houses and their faint lights.

Manuel told us when to stop. It wasn't just in the middle of nowhere; it was in the middle of a pitch-black, sloppy, muddy nowhere. We slid the box out and began our trek to Manuel's house. He and Sr. Mari, holding a flashlight, led the way. Fr. Vincent and I carried the coffin, hoisting it above our heads as we crossed through a deep culvert filled with rushing water. Then, after climbing up the other side, we crossed a field in pure blackness except for the flashlight's faint beam.

After a couple hundred yards Manuel told us to stop. We had arrived. He lived in the field. His house, made of sugarcane and pine branches woven together, had no lights, no driveway, no address. As the beam of the flashlight splashed against the tiny structure, I could see a small opening in the curved roof and a wisp of smoke.

Fr. Vincent and I got down on our knees to shove the box inside the house. We eased it alongside the body of Manuel's wife, which was lying on the wet earth in the one-room hut. A small fire was burning on the floor. It was mostly a handful of embers, but the occasional flicker of flame showed that the woman had been in her midthirties.

I can't tell you her name; I never learned it.

With difficulty, Fr. Vincent and I lifted her to place her in the casket. Not accustomed to this kind of face-to-face encounter with a dead body, I was startled by the gurgling of fluids as we lowered her into the box. As the pastor began to slide one end of the coffin lid toward me, a young boy slipped between us. I hadn't seen him in the semidarkness; my attention had been fixed upon the dead woman.

The young son was saying good-bye to his mother. He gently straightened out the woman's hair, wiped the moisture and bits of mud from her face, and kissed her on the forehead. No one moved as he took a *petate*—a light bedroll—and laid it over her in a simple but profound gesture of love and farewell. Fr. Vincent and I resumed positioning the lid and used rocks from the field to pound the nails into place. We later learned that on the following day, prisoners from a nearby jail were escorted out to the field to dig a grave and bury her.

That evening was a sacred moment for me. That mud floor was holy ground. Even today I remain touched by the tenderness with which the boy caressed his mother's face in one last gesture of love. I remain moved by this young woman's slipping away from this world so quietly.

Since that evening I've been comforted by the thought that although she was a stranger to even the people who lived in Ocosingo, she was known and loved by God. Since that evening I have thought of that bedroll; I have remembered that box.

Years later I served as a pastor in Los Angeles and attended or presided at many burials at some of the most exclusive cemeteries in the world, the final resting place for some of the world's most famous people.

But even as I stood in those lush settings, surrounded by ornate and expensive statuary, my mind returned to that field in Mexico. My hand again felt the rock I had used to pound those nails. Not a sparrow falls from the tree without the Father's knowing it, Jesus told us. That little sparrow—that wife, that mother, that woman whose name I never heard—*is* known and loved by God. He cherishes her. She is wrapped in a *petate* of infinite love.

Kaddish

Brian Doyle

from *Leaping: Revelations & Epiphanies*

Kaddish L'anashim: Prayers for Dead Men

The man who just liked to read the newspaper quietly.
The man who loved to preserve tomatoes.
The man whose two-year-old son was mortally ill.
The man who slept with his two dogs.
The man who occasionally vacuumed his lawn.
The man who was building a dollhouse for his daughter.
The man who was assistant treasurer at his church.
The man who helped found a church in New Jersey.
The man who was the best probationary fireman ever.
The man who built tiny ceramic railroad towns for his
    daughters.
The man who built forty crossbows.
The fireman who died with his fireman son.
The fireman who died with his fireman brother.
The fireman who died with his policeman brother.
The fireman who ran in with his fireman brother, who
    survived.

The fireman who hugged his fireman brother before
        entering the towers.
The man who had ten children, the youngest an infant.
The man who loved Cole Porter.
The man who loved Bruce Springsteen.
The man who loved Abba.
The man who loved The Who.
The man who was identified by his Grateful Dead tattoo.
The man who loved model trains.
The man who loved surfing.
The man who loved the Denver Broncos.
The man who loved the Detroit Lions.
The man who loved his racehorses.
The man who loved to run at night.
The man who loved to fish for striped bass.
The man who fished for bluefish from his lawn.
The man who loved his boxer dogs.
The man who loved fine red wine.
The man who loved Stolichnaya vodka on the rocks.
The man who loved skyscrapers.
The man who loved birdhouses.
The man who loved Les Paul guitars.
The man who loved dominoes.
The man who loved comic books.
The man who was rebuilding a 1967 Mustang.
The man who rebuilt a 1967 Mustang.
The man who was rebuilding a 1948 Studebaker.
The man who was rebuilding an MG convertible.
The man who restored an old hotel.
The man who started a ska band.
The man who built harpsichords.
The man who had been a model.
The man who could ski like the wind.

The man who drove a taxi as a hobby.

The man who drove blind women to church on Sunday.

The man who delivered papers every morning before going to work as a cook.

The man who meticulously rotated the socks in his drawer for even use.

The man who liked to handicap horse races.

The man who wasn't a saint by any means, according to his mom.

The man who was the youngest county treasurer in Missouri history.

The man who liked to cook kielbasa.

The man who liked to cook pinto beans.

The man who liked to cook meatloaf.

The man who liked to paint his daughters' fingernails.

The man who made a thousand paper cranes for his wife.

The man who made tea for his wife every day.

The man who cooked for his blind mother as a child.

The man with his mom's name tattooed on his arm.

The man with a bulldog tattooed on his arm.

The man who had *Death before Shame* tattooed on his arm in Gaelic.

The man who really wanted to go to Egypt.

The man who had been a boxer in Britain.

The man who had been a private detective.

The man who had been a cricket star in Guyana.

The man who had been a basketball star in the army.

The man who had been a lacrosse star in Australia.

The man who had been a lacrosse star in America.

The man who had been a hockey star in Canada.

The man who had been a hockey star in America.

The man who was an expert surfer.

The man who carried a surfboard everywhere.

The man who was a quadriplegic and typed with his mouth.
The fireman who played the bagpipes.
The fireman who played the piccolo.
The fireman who played the pennywhistle.
The man who made tea and toast for his wife every
      morning.
The man who hung out the flag with his daughter every
      morning.
The man who made wine in his basement.
The man who knew everything about boats.
The man who fixed his son's toy boat in the basement the
      night before.
The man who liked to quote Federico Fellini about the
      passion of life.
The man who was slowly going blind.
The man who bought bagels for everyone all the time.
The man who tied fly-fishing flies with his daughter.
The man who drew cartoons and caricatures of his friends.
The man who went to thirty-five Bruce Springsteen
      concerts.
The man who went to Mass every morning before boarding
      the train.
The man who cared for his kid sister with cerebral palsy.
The man who was a minister at House of God Church
      Number 1.
The man who was an elder at the Kingdom Hall of Jehovah's
      Witnesses.
The man who served two kinds of caviar at football tailgates.
The man who mounted a telescope on a sewer pipe in his
      yard.
The man who was married in full Scottish regalia.
The man who spoke Portuguese at home so his children
      would know the language.

The man who carried an old lifeguard from his wheelchair into the ocean for a last swim.

The man who carried a woman and her wheelchair down fifty floors to the street.

The man who was deaf and had been a furrier in the old country.

The man who was deaf and knew everyone in town.

The man who sat with the girl no one liked in high school.

The man who invited a mentally retarded girl to sit at the football players' table.

The man who flew small airplanes on Sunday mornings.

The man whose first son was born the day after he died.

The man whose first son was born a week after he died.

The man whose first son was born two weeks after he died.

The man whose first son was born three weeks after he died.

The man whose daughter announced her engagement two days before.

The man who wrote a song about noodles with his daughter.

The man who cleaned his neighbors' gutters.

The man whose parents were deaf.

The man whose parents had survived the Holocaust.

The man whose identical twin survived.

The man who once painted his black dog white.

The man who was a professor of geography.

The man from Cut Bank, Montana.

The man who dressed up like Elvis for his daughters.

The man who wanted to coach high school basketball.

The man who wanted to be a fly-fishing guide in Montana.

The man who shoveled snow for his pregnant neighbor.

The man who shoveled snow for old neighbors.

The man who called his mother every morning at 9:00 sharp.

The man who called his father every day after his mother died.
The man who called his wife three times a day.
The man who called his wife every day after lunch for
        fourteen years.
The man who left notes on the breakfast table every
        morning for his son.
The man who fixed a television transmitter with his shoelaces.
The man who coached every baseball player in his town for
        ten years.
The man who was working overtime to save money for his
        daughter's birthday.
The man who met his wife at a production of *Romeo and
        Juliet*.
The man whose wife found out she was pregnant after he
        died.
The man who helped his wife down eighty-eight floors and
        then went back in.
The man who boated down the Mekong River.
The man who rescued children from a day-care center that
        morning.
The man who rescued infant twins from a burning building.
The man who rescued an elderly couple from a burning
        building.
The man who carried a man from a burning building.
The man who carried a woman down seventy flights of stairs
        in the 1993 bombing.
The fireman who carried a paralyzed child on a tour of the
        station house.
The man who delivered a baby in an ambulance.
The man who carried toys with him for distraught children
        on his paramedic calls.
The man who carried dog biscuits in his pockets everywhere
        he went.

The man whose dog cried all night long for two weeks
afterward.

The man who mowed the Little League field with his own
lawn mower.

The man who had just taught his son to whistle.

The man who taught his pet bird to whistle.

The man who had just taught his daughter to dribble a
basketball.

The man who had just signed up for his first college class.

The man who went to college classes every night.

The fireman who was also a substitute teacher at the junior
high.

The fireman who accidentally burned down his own firehouse.

The man who wore photographs of his children on a
necklace.

The man who still did cannonballs when he jumped in the
pool.

The man who had been homeless for years but finally had a
job.

The man whose job started the day before.

The man whose job started two days before.

The man who started his own carpet-cleaning company.

The man who grilled ribs in winter while wearing a parka.

The man who loved to catch crayfish in his creek.

The man who raised racing pigeons.

The man who carried his failing wife everywhere in his arms.

The man whose police shield is in President Bush's pocket.

Kaddish L'nashim: Prayers for Dead Women

The woman who loved her two dogs.

The woman who loved her three dogs.

The woman who loved really strong coffee.
The woman who was a firefighter.
The woman who loved to ride her bike in the desert.
The woman whose job started the day before.
The woman whose name meant *love* and *joy* in Yoruba.
The woman whose sons were named Oz and Elvis.
The woman who raised llamas.
The woman who taught karate to deaf children.
The woman who taught every Sunday at Holy Rosary School.
The woman with piercing hazel eyes.
The woman with a famous giggle.
The woman who sang lead soprano at church.
The woman who played piano for opera troupes.
The woman who loved dancing to the Violent Femmes.
The woman who loved everything British.
The woman who fought the bully in school.
The woman you could count on for anything.
The woman who was raised by missionaries in Japan.
The woman who prayed the rosary with the pope.
The woman whose son was autistic.
The woman whose identical twin survived.
The woman who had been homeless.
The woman who brought clothes to homeless mothers.
The woman who died with her nephew.
The woman who died with her brother.
The woman who died with her husband and brother.
The woman who toured the country singing with
        Duke Ellington.
The woman who wanted to open a flower shop.
The woman who collected angels.
The woman who listened with her fullest attention.
The woman who fed sparrows every morning in her backyard.
The woman who gave her place on the elevator away that
        morning.

The woman who was the craziest chocolate person ever.
The woman who called her dad every day.
The woman who loved pedicures on Saturday mornings.
The woman who had just quit smoking.
The woman who first kissed her husband under the twin
        towers.
The woman who died with her husband on the 104th floor.
The woman who had planned everything about her wedding
        except the invitations.
The woman who wrote fifty-five-word short stories.
The woman who wrote her will the day before.
The woman who sketched commuters on the train every
        morning.
The woman who was seven months pregnant.
The woman who discovered that morning that she was
        pregnant.

Kaddish L'yiladim v'yiladot: Prayers for Dead Boys and Girls

The boy who wanted to be an ambulance driver.
The girl, age four, flying with her mother.
The boy, age three, flying with his parents.
The child inside the woman who was seven months pregnant.
The children inside mothers who didn't know of them yet.
The children who would have been conceived in years to
        come.
Their children, and their children's children.
May they swim in the sea of Light forever.

Contributors

John L. Allen Jr. covers the Vatican for the *National Catholic Reporter* newspaper and analyzes Vatican affairs for CNN. His articles have appeared in the *New York Times,* the *Irish Examiner,* and the *Tablet,* among other publications, and he is the author of *Cardinal Ratzinger: The Vatican's Enforcer of the Faith; Conclave: The Politics, Personalities, and Process of the Next Papal Election;* and, most recently, *All the Pope's Men: The Inside Story of How the Vatican Really Works.*

Scott Appleby is a professor of history at the University of Notre Dame, where he also directs the Joan B. Kroc Institute for International Peace Studies. He directed the Cushwa Center for the Study of American Catholicism from 1993 to 2002 and was codirector (with Lutheran theologian and author Martin Marty) of the Fundamentalism Project, an international public-policy study conducted by the American Academy of Arts and Sciences, from 1988 to 1993. Appleby is the author or editor of a number of books about American Catholicism and fundamentalism, among them *The Ambivalence of the Sacred: Religion, Violence, and Reconciliation* and (with Jay Dolan) *Transforming Parish Ministry: The Changing Roles of Catholic Clergy, Laity, and Women Religious.* Appleby lives in Granger, Indiana, with his wife, Peggy, and their four children.

Ben Birnbaum is the editor of *Boston College Magazine,* director of that Jesuit university's marketing communications office, and counselor to its president. His writings have been published in such journals as *TriQuarterly* and *Midstream Magazine,* and his essay "How to Pray: Reverence, Stories, and the Rebbe's Dream," first published in *Image,* is included in *Best American Essays 2001.* Birnbaum is married with three children and lives in Massachusetts.

Murray Bodo, OFM, is a Franciscan friar and member of the Franciscan Academy. The author of more than twenty books, which include *Landscape of Prayer* and the best-selling *Francis: The Journey and the Dream,* Fr. Bodo is also a published poet and former teacher of English and writing. He lives in the oldest Franciscan community in the country, in Cincinnati, Ohio.

Lawrence Cunningham is the John A. O'Brien Professor of Theology at the University of Notre Dame. A scholar especially of the history and practice of Catholic spirituality, he is author or editor of seventeen books, among them *Thomas Merton and the Monastic Vision.* For ten years he has written book reviews for *Commonweal* magazine, and he has been honored three times by the Catholic Press Association (1987, 1999, and 2000). He and his wife, Cecilia, have two daughters.

Christopher de Vinck is the author of eleven books, including the best-selling *Power of the Powerless: A Brother's Legacy of Love* and *Finding Heaven: Stories of Going Home.* His articles and essays have appeared in the *Wall Street Journal* and *Reader's Digest,* among other publications, and he frequently speaks at conferences and retreats across the country. A former high school English teacher, he is a public-school administrator in Pompton Plains, New Jersey, where he lives with his wife, Rosemary, and their three children.

Brian Doyle is the editor of *Portland Magazine* at the University of Portland and the author of four essay collections, most recently *Leaping: Revelations & Epiphanies. Two Voices: A Father and Son Discuss Family and Faith,* his collection with his father, Jim Doyle, won a Christopher Award and a Catholic Press Association Book Award. Brian Doyle's essays have appeared in the Best American Essays collections of 1998, 1999, and 2003. He is also the editor of *God Is Love,* a collection of the best spiritual essays from the pages of *Portland Magazine.* Doyle lives in Oregon with his wife and three children.

Paul Elie, an editor at Farrar, Straus and Giroux in New York, is the author of *The Life You Save May Be Your Own: An American Pilgrimage* and the editor of *A Tremor of Bliss: Contemporary Writers on the Saints.* He has been a contributor to *Commonweal,* the *New Republic,* and other magazines.

Diane Filbin is a writer who lives in Chicago, where she is a research manager at an investment bank. Her articles have appeared in *Commonweal* and the *National Catholic Reporter.*

Mary Ann Glendon is the Learned Hand Professor of Law at Harvard University Law School. She is an internationally renowned voice on bioethics and human rights and is the author of many books, among them *A World Made New: Eleanor Roosevelt and the Universal Declaration of Human Rights* and *Rights Talk: The Impoverishment of Political Discourse.* She is also a frequent contributor to *First Things.* A resident of Chestnut Hill, Massachusetts, she and her husband are the parents of three daughters.

Dominic Grassi is an urban priest, a natural storyteller, and the author of the *Bumping into God* books. A lifelong Chicagoan, Fr. Grassi has been a coach, a counselor, a retreat and vocation director, and an inspirational speaker. His most recent book is *Still Called by Name: Why I Love Being a Priest.*

Andrew Greeley, a priest of the Archdiocese of Chicago, teaches at the University of Chicago and the University of Arizona. He is the author of more than fifty books, many of them best-selling novels, including *Bishop Goes to the University* and *The Catholic Imagination.* He has written hundreds of scholarly and popular articles and writes a column for the *Chicago Sun-Times.* His latest book is *Catholic Revolution: New Wine, Old Wineskins, and the Second Vatican Council.*

Patrick Hannon, CSC, is the president of Notre Dame High School in Niles, Illinois. His essays have appeared in *U.S. Catholic,* among other magazines, and in the collections *Christmas Presence: Twelve Gifts That Were More Than They Seemed* and *Hidden Presence: Twelve Blessings That Transformed Sorrow or Loss.*

Paul Mariani is a professor of literature and writing at Boston College and the author of many books of poetry (among them *The Great Wheel* and *Salvage Operations*), biography and commentary (among them books about William Carlos Williams, Gerard Manley Hopkins, Hart Crane, and Robert Lowell), and spiritual adventure, including his two most recent tomes, *Thirty Days: On Retreat with the Exercises of St. Ignatius* and *God and the Imagination: On Poets, Poetry, and the Ineffable.* He and his wife, Eileen, have three sons and live in western Massachusetts.

James Martin, SJ, is an associate editor of *America* magazine in New York and the author of *Searching for God at Ground Zero; In Good Company: The Fast Track from the Corporate World to Poverty, Chastity, and Obedience;* and *This Our Exile: A Spiritual Journey* *with the Refugees of East Africa,* among other books. He has written for a number of publications and is the editor of *Awake My Soul: Contemporary Catholics on Traditional Devotions,* a collection of essays from the pages of *America.*

Alice McDermott is the author of five novels, most recently *Child of My Heart.* Her fourth novel, *Charming Billy,* won the 1998 National Book Award for fiction; her second novel, *That Night,* was made into a Warner Brothers film. She has twice been a finalist for the Pulitzer prize in fiction. Her short fiction has appeared in *Seventeen* and *Redbook,* among other magazines, and her nonfiction has been published in the *New York Times* and the *Washington Post.* McDermott is the Macksey Professor in the Writing Seminars at Johns Hopkins University in Baltimore. She lives in Bethesda, Maryland, with her husband and their three children.

Kathleen Norris is a poet, essayist, and writer whose memoirs *Dakota: A Spiritual Geography* and *The Cloister Walk* are bestsellers. She has been published in a number of magazines and journals, including the *New Yorker* and the *New York Times Magazine.* Her works also include seven poetry collections, the book *Amazing Grace: A Vocabulary of Faith,* and her most recent book, *The Virgin of Bennington,* a memoir of her love affair with New York City. Norris and her husband live in Lemmon, South Dakota.

John O'Callaghan is a professor of philosophy at the University of Notre Dame. He is the author of *Thomistic Realism and the Linguistic Turn: Toward a More Perfect Form of Existence* and is the coeditor (with Thomas Hibbs) of *Recovering Nature: Essays in Natural Philosophy, Ethics, and Metaphysics in Honor of Ralph McInerny.*

Ferdinand Oertel studied at Saint Louis University in Missouri after World War II and earned his doctorate in American literature from the University of Cologne. Now retired, he was long the editor in chief of *Leben & Frziehen* (*To Live and Educate*), a German Catholic magazine, in which capacity he was elected president of the German Catholic Press Association and the International Federation of Associations of Church Press. He is the author of *Jugend im Feuerofen* (*Ordeal by Fire*), a study of German Catholic youth in the Hitler era. He was named a Knight of Saint Gregory for his service to the church by His Holiness Pope John Paul II. He lives in Aachen, Germany.

Robert T. Reilly was a freelance writer who lived in Omaha, Nebraska. He wrote a number of books, including *Irish Saints;* hundreds of articles, essays, and short stories; documentary film and television scripts; and poetry. For fifteen years he was a professor of communications, creative writing, and Irish literature at the University of Nebraska-Omaha.

Paul Scanlon, OP, is pastor of St. Christopher by the Sea Church in Unalaska, in the Aleutian Islands of Alaska. He has served as a missionary in Mexico and at parishes in Los Angeles and Anchorage and has been the formation director and provincial for the Western Dominican Province. He is currently working on a book, from which the essay here is taken, *Treasures from the Poor in Spirit*.

Valerie Schultz is a freelance writer and director of religious education in Tehachapi, California. Her essays and articles have appeared in a number of publications, including *Mothering,* the *Los Angeles Times, America,* and *Sojourners,* and she is a columnist for the *Bakersfield Californian.* She and her husband are the parents of four daughters.

Gary Smith, SJ, is a Jesuit priest of the Oregon Province. His stories of living and working in the poverty-stricken Old Town section of Portland were collected in the book *Radical Compassion: Finding Christ in the Heart of the Poor.* He is currently working with the Jesuit Refugee Service in Uganda.

Margaret O'Brien Steinfels was the editor of *Commonweal* magazine from 1988 to 2002 and is the former editor of both *Christianity and Crisis* magazine and *Church,* the journal of the National Pastoral Life Center. She is the author of *Who's Minding the Children?:The History and Politics of Day Care in America* and is the editor of *American Catholics and Civic Engagement: A Distinctive Voice* and *American Catholics, American Culture: Tradition and Resistance.* Her articles and essays appear in a wide variety of Catholic and secular journals, among them the *New Republic* and the *Los Angeles Times.* She and her husband, Peter, live in New York and are the parents of two children.

Judith Valente, an award-winning journalist, published poet, and former writer for the Chicago and London bureaus of the *Washington Post* and *Wall Street Journal,* is an on-air correspondent for the PBS series *Religion and Ethics NewsWeekly.* A two-time finalist for the Pulitzer prize in journalism, Valente has had her poems published in *Rhino, AfterHours,* and *TriQuarterly,* among other journals. She lives in Chicago.

Mary Vineyard is a writer, massage therapist, and mother of two who lives in Lubec, Maine. Her essays and poems appear regularly in the *National Catholic Reporter.*

Gregory Wolfe is editor and publisher of *Image: A Journal of the Arts and Religion* and director of the Center for Religious Humanism, both at Seattle Pacific University, where he is writer in residence. He is the author or editor of several books, among them *Malcolm Muggeridge: A Biography* and (with his wife, Suzanne) *Circle of Grace: Praying with—and for—Your Children.* His essays, reviews, and articles have appeared in *Commonweal, First Things,* and the *National Review,* among other publications. He and his wife are the parents of four children.

Ann Wroe is the special features editor for the *Economist* magazine and a columnist for the *Tablet.* She is the author of the award-winning *Pontius Pilate* and of *The Perfect Prince,* about a fifteenth-century claimant to the English throne. She lives in London with her husband and their three sons.

Acknowledgments

From Brian Doyle, editor, *The Best Catholic Writing 2004*

Loyola Press's Best Catholic Writing is an annual collection, and all manner of written work concerning Catholic life is eligible for inclusion in the next volume, *Best Catholic Writing 2005*. I will consider all writing that is true, remarkable, and Catholic-minded in the largest possible sense.

Please send me any articles, essays, poems, short stories, plays, speeches, sermons, elegies, eulogies, monologues, rants, raves, etc., that have been written or published in 2003 or 2004. I will also consider book excerpts and yet-to-be-published writings.

Send nominated entries to me by fax, e-mail attachment, or snail mail at

Brian Doyle
Portland Magazine
University of Portland
5000 N. Willamette Boulevard
Portland, OR 97203
bdoyle@up.edu
503 943 7202 phone
503 943 7178 fax